THE MAN THEY WANTED ME TO BE

ALSO BY JARED YATES SEXTON

The People Are Going to Rise Like the Waters Upon Your Shore:
A Story of American Rage

THE MAN THEY WANTED ME TO BE

Toxic Masculinity and a Crisis of Our Own Making

JARED YATES SEXTON

COUNTERPOINT
Berkeley, California

The Man They Wanted Me to Be

Library of Congress Cataloging-in-Publication Data
Names: Sexton, Jared, author.
Title: The man they wanted me to be : toxic masculinity and a crisis of our
    own making / Jared Yates Sexton.
Description: First hardcover edition. | Berkeley, California : Counterpoint,
    [2019]
Identifiers: LCCN 2018051327 | ISBN 9781640091818
Subjects: LCSH: Sexton, Jared. | Authors, American—21st century—Biography.
    | Journalists—United States—Biography. | Men—Socialization—United
    States. | Masculinity—United States.
Classification: LCC PS3619.E9835 Z46 2019 | DDC 818/.603 [B]—dc23
LC record available at https://lccn.loc.gov/2018051327

Jacket design by Matt Dorfman
Book design by Jordan Koluch

COUNTERPOINT
2560 Ninth Street, Suite 318
Berkeley, CA 94710
www.counterpointpress.com

Printed in the United States of America
Distributed by Publishers Group West

10 9 8 7 6 5 4 3 2 1

This book is dedicated to my mother, Patti Ann McKee
For all that we went through, and for never giving up

We do a great disservice to boys in how we raise them. We stifle the humanity of boys. We define masculinity in a *very* narrow way. Masculinity is a hard, small cage, and we put boys inside this cage.

—CHIMAMANDA NGOZI ADICHIE,
We Should All Be Feminists

CONTENTS

THE MAN THEY WANTED ME TO BE

Prologue

During the two years I reported from the 2016 campaign trail, I watched stump speeches in cramped union halls and polished addresses to thousands, survived the major conventions, dodged flash bangs and retreated from burning limos at an inaugural riot, and generally dove headfirst into one of the most bizarre and contentious political contests in American history. The majority of this time, however, was devoted to studying the phenomenon that was the Donald Trump campaign, a rolling disaster equal parts professional wrestling and pure rage. After sneaking into his rallies, speaking with his supporters, and examining that mess from every conceivable angle, what I eventually found, at the dark heart of it all, was white men.

At the rallies they'd crowd into a scrum in front of the stage and stand shoulder to shoulder. On their way in they'd buy buttons calling Hillary Clinton a "bitch," or else they'd choose between two of the most popular shirts for sale: "Hillary Sucks, But Not Like

Monica" or one with Trump riding a motorcycle that Clinton had just been thrown from and wearing a vest that said, "If you can read this the bitch fell off." In the comfort of the crowd they used disgusting language and trafficked in casual racism, virulent misogyny, and undisguised homophobia. At times, they seemed spurred on by each other, as if in competition to see who could step furthest over the line of common decency.

I was able to be one of the first journalists to walk among them because these are my people. Growing up in a dirt-poor factory family in southern Indiana, I'd heard all of this before, though usually behind closed doors, and thus could observe without flinching or revealing myself. I also knew how to dress—jeans, t-shirts, scuffed boots, an old, soiled baseball cap—and to carry myself as if I had better things to do and yet was ready to fight at a moment's notice. I could blend in because I'd been doing so for years, faking it with my own family. The things those men said I'd heard at barbecues and holidays. The same groups they were angry with were the ones they'd railed about for as long as I could remember.

These men raised me. They punished me when I didn't fit in. They beat me and tortured me, all in an effort to toughen me up and make me just like them. They were my uncles, my cousins, my friends, my neighbors, my stepfathers, and even my own father.

There in the crowd I looked and performed like them, but I still felt as strange and as odd as I did back home. From the time I was very little, I'd always been like a stranger among my family. I watched them and took my cues, but I could never escape the suspicion that in some way, shape, or form, I was unusual.

That fact didn't go unnoticed by the men in my world. To my relatives I was "different," a word I'd heard them use in a suspicious voice whenever they thought I was out of earshot. They were uncomfortable around me, thrown off by how I spoke and how often

I'd ask questions that required more than a monosyllabic "yes" or "no," or one of their customary grunts or groans women had learned to translate out of necessity. I talked about feelings, read books, and when I played with my toys, even the action figures and robots that all came with missiles and machine guns, they spent more time communicating than battling each other.

The patriarchal structure my family operated under was described by the women as "the way it's always been," a tired nod to a way of life that'd been rooted in place since before they were born. It meant that women tended to the home, even as they worked jobs to make ends meet, and then raised their children. The man was expectantly beleaguered by his backbreaking job, and having given his all to the factory, mine, or body shop, he had no more energy to spare for his partner or his family, no more strength for functioning besides maybe taking out the trash or mowing the yard on the weekend.

Men were effectively the kings of their household, the final word on every matter, above reproach or question. They were to be feared and taken care of. They sat in front of a game on the TV like a royal contemplating stately matters upon a throne. And like many kings, they possessed a great ability to be cruel. When their power or sovereignty was questioned, their response was anger. They yelled, they threw things, they were violent, and these outbursts always coincided with lapses in authority, humiliations at work, and any number of breaches of that sovereignty.

Like kings, they were also benefactors of privilege they had earned by simply being born. And when those privileges were tested—whether these were my relatives or the men like those at Trump's rallies—they declared war.

When I think about masculinity, and particularly my struggle to find my place in the masculine world, the man who comes to mind most is my father. Of course, father issues are nothing new—art is littered with books and songs and plays and movies about it—but when I look at my relationship with John Robert Sexton, those difficulties mostly center on what is expected out of a man.

Like the others, Dad knew I was different. Five years after he died, I sat down to talk with my stepmother, Nancy, and the word she used to describe his feelings about me as a child was "soft," a catchall that meant sensitive, vulnerable, artistic.

Following a traumatic and abusive divorce, my parents were estranged, and I spent the overwhelming majority of my time with my mom. I saw Dad on holidays and the occasional vacation, but I got a sense I made him uneasy and, over time, that he was happier when our time together was sparse.

When I did see him, though, I was terrified of his macho act. He bragged incessantly about his time in the Marines and preferred to be outside drinking beer and working with his hands. In his absence the family told stories about his legendary days raising hell. He had no time for my bullshit, and when we talked, which wasn't often, he was dismissive, sexist, racist, and closed off.

Back then, my dad would have been the exact type of man you'd expect to vote for Donald Trump.

When talk with his buddies turned to outsiders, be they immigrants, homosexuals, feminists, or the few African Americans or Mexicans who dared to move into our small Indiana town, things turned ugly. Like the conversations I'd heard in and outside Trump rallies, it was "our" town, "our" country. There was no doubt white men ruled the world and everyone else was looking to steal it away.

The older I got, and the more the distance between my dad and me started to hurt, I tried to play the role he expected. I'd go fishing, camping, bowling; I would stand there as he and the other men talked. Much like Donald Trump's infamous locker room session where he bragged that he could grab women "by the pussy," men unencumbered by the presence of women often break their self-imposed vow of silence, and what they say, more often than not, is beyond offensive.

I've heard men joke about wanting to rape women.

I've heard men describe their sexual encounters in stark, humiliating detail.

I've heard men use every slur, racial or otherwise, you could ever imagine.

I've heard men express their most fundamentally racist and sexist beliefs, have heard them lust after authoritarian power, say they'd be just fine eliminating all minorities, that they wish every man, woman, and child in the Middle East would be incinerated with nuclear bombs, have heard them discuss the merits of reinstituting slavery, and go several rounds of admiring Adolf Hitler.

For those men, communication is either a utility to get something done or another opportunity to further the illusion that they are unburdened by consciences or weak emotions.

My dad was like that for the majority of the thirty years I knew him. At nearly every occasion he was either stoic or aggressively politically incorrect, and the worldview he presented was as cold and cruel as he would like to have been perceived.

But then something happened.

He changed. Wholesale. When I look back on it I wonder if it was because he knew he was running out of time. Unchecked diabetes—like many men, Dad refused to tell anyone he was sick and then avoided seeing a doctor for fear of appearing weak—took his life at the early age of fifty-nine. But before it did, Dad spent the last decade of his life as a different man.

This came after we finally got to know each other and grew into friends. I was older and a few rough years had worn away some of the softness he'd despised in me. We met somewhere in the middle: me turning into a harder, stoic man and my father finally emerging from his shell.

In these years we did the tried-and-true masculine things. We watched ball games on the TV, fished for catfish and bluegill in stripper pits in the Greene-Sullivan State Forest, shot guns, stood out in the garage, as is customary, and generally bullshitted. But what was most amazing, other than my father's apparent transformation, was that Dad, seemingly exhausted by years of near-silence, began to speak openly about the burden of masculinity.

He told me the expectations he'd carried, as a father, as a son, as a man, had sabotaged his relationships and prevented him from expressing himself, or really enjoying intimacy, emotionally or intellectually, his entire life.

Shocked at the depth of frustration and despair my dad had suffered, I listened and realized, for the first time, that the masculinity I'd sought, the masculinity I'd been denied, had always been an impossibility. Deep down, I realized that masculinity, as I knew it, as it was presented to me, was a lie.

Men like my father, and men like him who attend Trump rallies, join misogynistic subcultures, populate some of the most hateful groups in the world, and are prisoners of toxic masculinity, an artificial construct whose expectancies are unattainable, thus making them exceedingly fragile and injurious to others, not to mention themselves. The illusion convinces them from an early age that men deserve to be privileged and entitled, that women and men who don't conform to traditional standards are second-class persons, are weak and thus detestable. This creates a tyrannical patriarchal system that tilts the world further in favor of men and, as a side effect, accounts for a great deal of crimes, including harassment, physical and emotional abuse, rape, and even murder.

These men, and the boys following in their footsteps, were socialized in childhood to exhibit the ideal masculine traits, including stoicism, aggressiveness, extreme self-confidence, and an unending competitiveness. Those who do not conform are punished by their fathers in the form of physical and emotional abuse, and then further socialized by the boys in their school and community who have been enduring their own abuse at home. If that isn't enough, our culture then reflects those expectations in its television shows, movies, music, and especially in advertising, where products like construction-site-quality trucks, power tools, beer, gendered deodorant, and even yogurt promise to bestow masculinity for the right price.

The masculinity that's being sold, that's being installed via systematic abuse, is fragile because, again, it is unattainable. Humans are not intended to suppress their emotions indefinitely, to always be confident and unflinching. Traditional masculinity, as we know it, is an unnatural state, and, as a consequence, men are constantly at war with themselves and the world around them.

––––––

This book is about all those things.

It's about the lie of traditional masculinity, its origins, the damage it has inflicted on men, women, children, and, ultimately, the world.

It's specifically about white patriarchal masculinity, an especially potent and toxic system of power and control that has subjugated women and minorities for generations via methodical and organized actions powered by misogyny and racism, a unique brand of maleness that held sway over the United States of America since before its founding.

It's about the men I grew up surrounded by, my family, my stepfathers, and my neighbors who abused and harassed and stalked and murdered.

It's about the societal, psychological, economic, and sociological consequences of a lie so pervasive and deep-rooted most people don't even know it's a lie.

It's about the current political impasse we find ourselves in where fragile white men with fragile manhoods have stalled social progress and propelled into the White House a tough-talking, thin-skinned vulgarian who embodies, more than anyone else, toxic American masculinity.

It's about how political polarization commoditized those insecurities while also cauterizing male doubt, thus creating a marketplace and a culture where insecure and embattled men engross themselves in products, entertainment, and a fabricated reality where the lie remains intact.

It's about labor and economics and a changing world where the jobs and societal forces that originally necessitated what has come to be known as the quintessential working-class American male have given way to a new era of progressivism that rewards communication, creativity, and education, all things that have been scorned in working-class families for generations.

It's about men who cherish independence and fashion themselves "self-made" while forces they either don't understand or aren't even aware of influence and shape them every single day of their lives.

It's about how complicated and exhausting masculinity is, how

ingrained and inescapable, how someone like myself, who was bullied and abused for his reluctance to conform, and even aware of
and educated about the lie, found himself, later in life, reacting to
crises by suddenly embodying the masculine traits he'd hated so
much, essentially becoming the man he'd feared his entire life and
finding himself in a bed in Muncie, Indiana, with the barrel of a
rifle in his mouth and a finger on the trigger.

And it's about how, after that close call, I decided to try, as im-
perfect as I am, to understand the lie and the people it hurt in an
effort to find another way to live.

I

A HARD, SMALL CAGE

1

On October 7, 2016, I was celebrating my thirty-fifth birthday when news broke that *The Washington Post* had just published an eleven-year-old video of Republican nominee Donald Trump telling *Access Hollywood* host Billy Bush about pursuing a married woman "like a bitch" and bragging that his status as a celebrity meant women let him do whatever he wanted, including grabbing them "by the pussy."

Reaction was swift. Prominent Republicans voiced their displeasure as pundits on cable news and the internet speculated that Trump would have to step away from the nomination. Though the billionaire had survived multiple scandals that would have buried any other politician, this seemed a step too far.

This was also the day Hurricane Matthew hit the southeastern United States. A few hours after the *Post* story dropped, Matthew slammed my home in Statesboro, Georgia, and torrential rain and violent winds buffeted my house well into the dawn. With the power out, I was left with a cooler full of beer and a night of deliberating whether Trump would drop out that evening or wait until the next day.

After a terrible, anxious sleep, I was woken up a little after 6:00 a.m. by a man at my door wearing a threadbare flannel and dry-rotted blue jeans. "You hire anyone to take care of the tree yet?" he asked, hooking his thumb toward my driveway, where a giant pine had toppled and just nearly missed destroying my car.

I took his number and told him I'd get back to him, and after he left I surveyed the damage in my yard and the neighborhood. Limbs and leaves littered the street. Other trees had been uprooted completely, their roots exposed and the holes left behind flooded with muddy water. Roofs everywhere were damaged, power lines sagged, cars flattened.

After a lap I came home to find my neighbor standing in my driveway and staring at the tree. A retired, older man, he'd always been quiet—the only words I'd ever heard from him were his dogs' names when he'd called them back to his yard. Not taking his eyes off the fallen tree, he asked, "You got a chainsaw?" When I told him I didn't he asked, "Why don't you have a chainsaw? You need one for stuff like this."

I explained that I'd bought the house, my first one, in April and was still working on getting the essentials.

"Huh."

Instantly I recognized the sound as one my male relatives had made so many times before.

And with that he walked back across the street, putting an end to our first conversation. By the time he returned with chainsaw in tow, I was feeling an old guilt I hadn't entertained in years: I'd failed at being a man.

My neighbor sawed into the trunk of the pine and for a while it seemed like he'd make quick and easy work of it until the blade caught in the meat of the tree. He braced himself with his boot on the bark and pulled to no avail. Frustrated, he backed off, put his hands on his hips, and sighed.

Not long after, other men who'd been surveying the damage joined us and grouped around my driveway the way men often do, in a half circle, their arms crossed or stuffed in their pockets, plenty of room between them.

With each new arrival they'd ask my neighbor what'd happened, if he'd tried this, tried that, then they'd take a turn trying to free the blade. Inevitably, they'd turn to me and ask whether I had a chainsaw, and when I said no, almost to a person, they'd answer with their own judgmental "Huh."

Later, after the saw had been rescued and the crowd dispersed, the man who'd knocked on my door that morning returned with a small crew that cut up the tree and left me a mess of limbs and logs to carry and roll out to the road. The manual labor felt good and had gone a long way toward restoring my bruised ego—that is, until I'd finished and just taken off my gloves, and one of the men from the earlier crowd came rolling by on a tricked-out golf cart, the kind that are very popular in my neighborhood, and when I raised my hand to wave I got in return a disapproving shake of the head.

For the next two days I went without power, meaning there was plenty of time to get lost in my thoughts and wonder how the fallout from the *Access Hollywood* tape was playing out. Every time I logged online I expected to find that Trump had dropped out of the race. Surprisingly, or maybe in retrospect not so surprisingly, Trump showed little remorse and even less intention to bow out. He dismissed the conversation as "locker room talk," a perfect description, honestly, as I'd heard just that kind of garbage in my years playing sports where I'd had to listen to teammates brag about their sexual conquests.

Even though it was a very small thing, the chainsaw situation stuck with me, and all of my time not spent analyzing Trump's unfailing lack of shame was dedicated to replaying the scene. I could still hear the confusion in those men's voices, could still see the annoyance on their faces.

I'd managed to leave my past life behind, a time I'd been different, unfamiliar and uncomfortable with the customs of men. Starting when I was nineteen, I'd changed and began carrying myself differently, dressed myself similarly, worked some jobs that earned calluses and supplemented the knowledge I was supposed to have learned when I was younger. With the new house I'd renovated portions of it, taught myself how through research and trial and error. To people who didn't know me before then, I appeared, for all intents and purposes, to be a pretty standard, working-class, midwestern man.

The incident with the saw reminded me of my shortcomings and got me thinking about my life and the culture in which someone like Donald Trump, a boisterous "man's man" who'd said he wanted protesters punched in the face, could survive a scandal like the release of the *Access Hollywood* tape. I jotted down some notes and began to see a pattern that seemed to be passing unnoticed in the conversation about just what the hell was going on.

I pitched my editor at *The New York Times* and wrote the first paragraph to an op-ed titled "Donald Trump's Toxic Masculinity."

My editorial hit a nerve as my inbox filled up with emails from men and women alike. Some of the men were angry and called me a "faggot" and questioned my testosterone count while others were thankful to hear they weren't alone in being suspicious of the tenets of masculinity. The article framed my father figures as the last of a dying breed of men who unnecessarily punished themselves and the world around them, and these men who reached out looked at the prior generation with a puzzlement similar to my own.

When women wrote they told me their own stories about their fathers, brothers, husbands, and sons and how they were enigmas to them, men who wouldn't communicate their feelings, their insecurities, their problems. Some said they'd been considering divorcing their husbands and some talked about the stress of raising a new generation to be better than the ones before.

But some of the women weren't as supportive. One wrote that I should be ashamed of myself. According to her, the piece was another in a long line of liberal attempts to emasculate America. In her last sentence she asked, "Whatever happened to men being men?"

What she was referring to was the arbitrary gender binary by which most Americans understand the world. To that reader, and many like her, there are men and there are women and they are to behave according to their expected roles. This is as simplistic and as self-evident as the sky's being blue and gravity's holding our feet to the ground. But gender is a social construct, a result of cultural influence and pressures that have developed over time into an assumed dichotomy, and it is because of those pressures exerted by society that we see gender roles as concrete as opposed to subjective states of being.

To understand this concept, one must first know from where modern traditional American masculinity originated—more specifically white, cisgender masculinity, which this book will focus on because the patriarchy that has controlled our culture has been defined and enforced by this group and includes tenets of societal privilege and white supremacy—and what necessitated both its origin and how it was adopted en masse as the status quo. Likewise, in modern times, it must be examined how these roles have been challenged by each successive generation, a reality that has led to what some have called the crisis of masculinity, a period of uncertainty and much consternation as to just what it means to be a man in America.

———

Often it is said that winners write history, and if that is true, and it most assuredly is, then my people have contributed very little to the canon. I am descended from a long line of peoples who have failed to overcome the terrible gravity of poverty.

Once upon a time my grandma Burk, my mother's mom, had retired and, looking for something to fill her time, decided to spend a summer researching our family's genealogy after a television ad for an early ancestry service piqued her interest. Grandma was an easy mark for TV products. A fervent devotee of Ron Popeil, the inventor and infomercial spokesperson for products like the Ronco Food Dehydrator and the Showtime Rotisserie, Grandma would buy in big and spend the days waiting for its delivery, fantasizing about how it would revolutionize her life. The dehydrator didn't live up to her expectations and, unsurprisingly, neither did the ancestry service.

Where Grandma had expected to find direct links to legendary figures like George Washington or Davy Crockett—according to familial lore both were distant relatives—what she found was a family tree stocked with scofflaws, debtors, drunkards, and out-and-out criminals. The experiment stopped abruptly after she found a succession of relatives who'd either been hung for horse thievery or killed in senseless barroom altercations.

Despite the promise of the American Dream, and an assurance that anybody can overcome their station in life, this country contains a lot of families like mine that never managed to escape the cycle of their predecessors' poverty. They're descended from men who worked in the factories and mines of yesteryear before they were closed and shuttered and replaced by jobs behind a fast-food counter and government assistance. They're beleaguered and depressed, worn out and pissed off. They've watched generations of their families work hard and never get any more reward than dying at an early age from exhaustion with bodies broken by labor.

The American Dream that spurred them on has its roots in both the founding of this country and its underlying principles. The United States is a nation of immigrants who fled their native lands in hopes of staking out better futures. It is a relatively new country whose revolution was fought on the idea of personal freedom and the rights of humans to seek their destinies. Imbedded in that ideal is the seed of permanent revolution, the concept of an ongoing experiment that continually reinvents itself and is thus boundless.

The promise of the new country, as well as its capitalistic underpinnings and the draw of Manifest Destiny, meant that the American Dream was achievable, but that those who hadn't experienced its bounty yet might be just one idea or one day away from striking it rich. This gave hope to my ancestors and others like them. They worked hard, or else hustled hard, and they emigrated from Europe to the colonies and then Indiana and beyond. They drove forward, these frontiersmen, and settled the American West in search of their fortunes until they hit the Pacific Ocean and found themselves still wanting.

With the American landscape tamed, and the country now spanning from sea to shining sea, the market represented a new horizon. With the Industrial Revolution, and a shift from agrarian culture to mechanization, the promise of self-made fortune was realized by giants like John D. Rockefeller, Cornelius Vanderbilt, Andrew Carnegie, and men like them who built the country as we know it and, in doing so, employed generations of men who worked in miserable conditions for subpar pay.

American masculinity and patriarchal society have roots that go back well past this time period. In fact, white American men have enjoyed privileges since before there was an America, and those privileges resulted in the overthrow of Native Americans, the enslavement of African Americans, mistreatment of minorities, the controlled subservience of women, and an order of hegemonic power that has existed well into the twenty-first century. It has defined the struggle of America since its conception.

But the masculinity we are most familiar with, that of the laborer and the breadwinner, grew into being following the Civil War, an apocalyptic battle that left hundreds of thousands dead and began the transformation of the United States from an agrarian society to an industrialized one. The surrendering of the Confederacy found the slaves freed and the financial order of the country upended, meaning the hegemonic patriarchy had been dealt a slow bleeding wound that would prove fatal generations later.

In the wake of this sea change our modern definition of masculinity was forged, a definition that has lasted for roughly a hundred and fifty years and is now being left behind.

The men who would comprise my family and countless others were laborers who toiled in workplaces devoid of joy and rampant with safety hazards. Before the advent of unions and labor rights movements, these were jobs where men were overworked, underpaid, and maimed regularly. It was hellish, and in order to go to work every day the laborer had to adapt both himself and his expectations to survive his harsh reality.

Faced with a job that paid just enough to keep a family afloat, and sometimes not even that, the American man adapted his idea of self-worth to depend on his identity as a laborer as opposed to his fulfillment of the American Dream. Callused hands and tired bones became indicators of self-worth and proof of an attempt, however futile, to do the necessary work to survive, if not advance.

What made this exchange possible was the laborer's status as a white male, a privileged position that, regardless of station or worth, prioritized him above women, minorities, homosexuals, and immigrants. He may have failed to advance or conquer the world as the Gods of Industry had, but society was in his favor and at home he was still king.

American economic expansion supported a generation of families who barely survived until the market crash of 1929 plunged the country into the Great Depression, a horrific event where families like mine struggled just to eat. My grandparents' childhoods were things of nightmares, and like anyone's who lived through the Depression, their stories are a stark reminder of the fragility of society. My great-grandparents were miners, limestone workers, handymen. When the bottom fell out, they found themselves the patriarchs of families that were homeless, starving, and beyond desperate.

Often called "The Greatest Generation," my grandparents belonged to an era dominated by a sense of duty where on the heels of a depression survival was the only goal. When World War II broke out, young men like my grandpa willingly joined the army and fought in the European Theater. Like many women, my grandma filled the absence of men who had left the factory floor for the battlefield and pitched in making war materials. They focused on a single existential crisis in the form of fascism. Personal ambition and pursuit of the American Dream would have to wait.

War's end found my grandpa returning home a wounded hero with post-traumatic stress disorder he soothed with the bottle. Grandma made room for the men in the factory and returned to her duties in the home. She told me with the Allied victory and the resulting postwar boom it finally felt like America was back on track, but unbeknownst to her another revolution was only beginning.

As Europe struggled to rebuild, America rode the economic boom and the fevered production of its factories outfitted to win a war, only now, instead of bombs, guns, equipment, and vehicles, production turned to hallmarks of advancing modernity, these weapons designed to win the battle of convenience. Assembly lines pumped out refrigerators, washers, dryers, TVs, and automobiles. Efficiency revolutionized production, but the individualized labor meant the men working the lines were removed even further from the finished product and their association and pride with their labor thus diminished.

The new economy changed everything. Women who once struggled with household duties were able to complete them with less effort and time, meaning they now had more precious hours to think, learn, consider their position in society's hierarchy, and elect to join the workforce. The veterans who had effectively saved the world now churned out products of postwar luxury, and their place on the line relegated them to being just another cog in a very massive machine.

With factories pumping out war-level streams of products Americans had yet to come to depend on, companies were forced to devise a way to sell them. This resulted in the birth of modern advertising. Built on the psychological theories of Sigmund Freud, advertisers used appeals to the unconscious needs and fears of the American consumer. Freud's own nephew, Edward Bernays, trailblazed this new approach that leveraged the mind against its owner in order to create new markets.

Soon, products and behaviors with no relation to gender were being imbued with male and female attributes and the unconscious insecurities for men and women, mainly that men could not live up to artificially created masculine roles and women could not achieve their inorganic expectations. These insecurities were exploited for financial gain and through careful framing and subconscious appeals these products were marketed as opportunities to supplement these concerns, an ingenious and insidious ploy, as gender expectations were always unachievable anyway.

This new arena fundamentally changed culture forever. In the past men and women could rely only on their families and communities as reflections on how they were faring in their adherence, but now, with the advent of mass media and anxiety fostered by advertising, their insecurities and fear of failure were multiplied as, according to their televisions, everyone else in the world was adhering to their roles. In addition, mass media reflected gender roles back to a society that then reflected them back onto mass media. Men watched John Wayne and saw the ideal man they tried to emulate. Veterans who'd survived World War II but had served in fear or

suffered PTSD as my grandfather had would then consume simplistic movies that portrayed them as fearless, unshakable warriors,
a portrayal the men in turn began to mirror.

In essence, American masculinity, or rather the lie of American
masculinity, became another product in the same vein as a fridge
from Whirlpool that cooled the family's groceries or the new Chevy
glimmering in the driveway of the suburban home.

Transactional advertising was just the beginning. The lie of
masculinity, an ancestor of the worldview that'd helped men survive torturous industry, proved politically advantageous for those
in power. Hazardous conditions and mistreatments by employers
had long been challenged by labor unions and movements, but in
the postwar period employers and controllers of industry under-
cut unions using masculine insecurities against laborers in the form
of "The Red Scare," or cultivated fear of Soviet infiltration. The
panic played on male insecurity as protectors of their family and
essentially convinced them to turn against their own interests in
exchange for continued propagation of the masculine role. This
worked then, much as it does now, because of the remaining identity of laborers and their worth being determined by their ability to
provide and protect.

In the absence of union influence, laborers like my family settled into a life where they were paid little, but their worth was based
on, and their insecurities salved by, continued consumerism. This
new stasis allowed the wealthy who owned the means of production to consolidate power and pad their wealth without the threat
of unionization or collective action. Over the successive years, the
gap between the laborers and the wealthy expanded at inconceivable speed, and whenever laborers began to show frustration with
their lot in life, or began to overcome their predilection for stylized
"rugged individualism" in favor of collective action, those old tactics

of fearmongering and playing upon the inherent insecurities made sure to put down any potential threat from organized labor.

This worked well for so very long, in part because the Greatest Generation had internalized a worldview where advancement was secondary to fulfillment of societal responsibilities. They also existed in a time where America's economy was still booming and a person could work nearly any job and fulfill the necessary requirements of a breadwinner. There were jobs for nearly everyone, and having one meant employment, more than likely for life, a guarantee that meant a car, a home, an education for their 2.5 children, and all the trimmings of an ideal American life. The lie survived as long as people could stay afloat and experience at least a slice of the American Dream.

In the postwar years, it seemed like the wave would never crest. Industry was humming due to its exploitation of its workers, and laborers enjoyed relative security. And then, the Baby Boomers came of age and cut their teeth on a thriving economy. They grew up with luxuries and a world that celebrated "the self," a by-product of consumerist culture that partnered the specter of fear with the promise of self-actualization. The Baby Boomers had one foot in the past, where duty and perseverance were most important, and one foot firmly in the future, where personal aspirations were all that mattered.

Men like those in this book were products of this crucial time. They were a new kind of American who grew up surrounded by tremendous social, economic, and technological progress and were thus terribly torn between the duty of their fathers and the emerging self. The battle between those diametrically opposed instincts, as well as the struggle for what the future would look like, would dominate society for the next half century. With the civil rights movement, the rise of feminism, a new technological revolution, and the slow death of male-centric occupations like manufacturing, agriculture, and labor, the long-maintained bedrock of the patriarchy was quickly coming apart at the seams.

The defeat of American interests in Vietnam would prove a turning point in our history, as the loss represented an emasculation the patriarchal culture has yet to get over, but the surrounding tumult and rise of the progressive counterculture in response to the war would challenge the hegemonic order in a manner yet before unseen. The antiwar movement and counterculture's progress might not have been apparent at the moment, but their reverberations continue to change the world.

Progress in the market made an unlikely ally in the battle against the patriarchy. Women entered the workforce out of economic need, but were thus able to find increasing measures of financial and personal independence. Minorities who'd been discriminated against were able to ply their trade without the overt interference of an ingrained systematic prejudice. Trade deals like the North American Free Trade Agreement heralded a shifting of priorities from labor-driven industry toward a newer, more humane economy wherein workers could make a living without sacrificing their bodies and their health.

While these were signs of progress, men reacted as if they themselves were threatened instead of the patriarchal order that imprisoned them. They doubled down on misogyny, discriminated against women in the workplace, blocked the upward mobility of anyone but themselves, opposed civil rights as corrective measures that would have improved the economy, and supported politicians who promised to oppose progress and swore to bring back the former economic order they had languished in their entire lives. This stunted progress and growth created a stagnant atmosphere in which rusted and regressive technologies and cultures stayed well past their expiration dates, and resulted in an America that was just as unprepared for the future as it was incapable of living in the past.

This limbo meant education became unaffordable and unappreciated, health care costs skyrocketed, wages stagnated, new energy alternatives were eschewed in favor of finite and polluting resources like oil and coal, mounting crises like global climate change went unchecked, and the last vestiges of the industrial past were clung to like so many boards from a sunken ship until there was nothing left to do but drown. Instead of progressing and changing, men caught in the patriarchy fell behind and pulled everyone down with them until they looked around, saw the mess they had made, and asked how things had gotten so bad.

The answer to that question is the backdrop of this story, which spans from the 1960s to the present day. As the events take place, the hegemonic order is beginning a collapse that has been in the making for decades, and as it progresses the changing economy is closing factories around the country, including ones in my small hometown of Linton, Indiana. Without alternative employment, investment, or training, the men losing their jobs were ripe to be manipulated into opposing progress. The structured and reliable existence men like my father and stepfathers had come to depend on is disappearing by the day and the realization that the world is changing is exerting massive amounts of pressure on these men, all of whom are already fragile in their masculinity and aggrieved in their entitlement. It's a story of men refusing to come to terms with their situation because to be a white man in America is to expect everything to already be on your terms.

Before any of the people mentioned in this book were ever born, this battle was already lost. The initial creation of the patriarchal structure doomed the system before it ever took hold because it's a fabricated state of being at odds with itself. The lie was always destined to fail, it was only a matter of when, and the date of the decline came soon after World War II, when the men of America were made to come as close to the masculine ideal as possible, and the mass culture and capitalistic system of the country depended on supplementing their faults and selling that supplementation to sons like my very own father, who were destined to come up short and rage against everyone and everything but the system that had let them down in the first place.

2

Last summer I drove back to Indiana to visit family and was feeling nostalgic before I'd even reached Linton's city limits. I'm always affected when I go home. It starts when the interstate gives way to the rural landscape with its farms and rolling hills, then the town with its abandoned storefronts and string of thriving churches. To drive through southern Indiana is to see an America that has been largely forgotten and has grown weary. While the 2016 presidential election raged and brought to surface all the frustrations and wrath that had been simmering for decades, thus ensuring Donald Trump would gain purchase, home haunted me with new meaning.

I was going to sit down with Nancy, my dad's second wife and widow, and when I crossed the old railroad tracks and got to her new place, situated just a few blocks away from the house where she'd lived with my dad for decades, it was sizzling hot and the neighborhood silent except the whine of overburdened air conditioners. After I'd parked she stepped outside and greeted me with a hug both warm and cautious.

"Guess you know who we're voting for, huh?" she said, nodding at the Trump/Pence sign swaying in the front yard.

In the weeks before, I'd been singled out by Trump supporters for my reporting, resulting in efforts to get me fired from my university job while others, mostly white supremacists, threatened to murder me in my home. On several occasions people had shown up at my door, tried to break into my house. Harassing letters were regularly arriving in the mail. Accordingly, the sign my own relatives proudly displayed still made me uncomfortable.

Honestly though, it wasn't the most uncomfortable part of my visit. After my dad had died in 2012, my stepmother, Nancy, had moved on and moved in with a man named Lonnie. Following her loss, she'd pulled together the pieces and formed a new life for herself. Seeing Nancy in a new setting was strange, and I could tell she'd tried to make for herself a new start.

"We're trying to live simply," she said, gesturing at rooms filled with family portraits, throw pillows, and rustic signs reading FAITH, FAMILY, FRIENDS. There were knickknacks and keepsakes, but it was definitely a change from life with Dad, who had always been a pack rat. Their house had been full of clutter and junk, and when he'd died Nancy had sorted through all of it, a full-time job in its own right, and had given me bags full of knives, guns, Beanie Babies he'd expected to balloon in value, Indiana basketball memorabilia, NASCAR collectibles, and a ring he'd claimed had been given to him by a girl the singer John Prine had allegedly proposed to.

The Prine ring was a bit of family lore, which my dad liked to spin yarns about at the table. Dad was a storyteller who relished every opportunity to glorify his adventures and hold the attention of an audience. According to Nancy, though, the biggest story my dad ever told had come in the years before his untimely death.

"Your dad was a proud man," Nancy told me once we'd settled into the back office to talk. "He was sick for years and wouldn't let you kids know. When it was just us, he could barely walk and hurt all the time. And then, when somebody would come around, he'd put on a big show."

The big show had convinced me for a while. When I'd visit, Dad would briefly mention what he called "arthritis" while he hobbled around and grimaced in obvious pain. We'd go and catch a high school football or basketball game and he'd seem fine, if not slowly succumbing to old age. That was before November 2011, when, early in the morning, I'd gotten a call that he'd been rushed to the hospital, and the big show had been convincing enough that I'd been completely blindsided.

In the harsh light of the waiting room that morning, Nancy had broken the bad news by saying, "This was a long time coming."

As Nancy talked about my dad's death in her new house with her new partner, I couldn't help but admire her. Like the other women in my life she'd put up with so much shit. She's tough. She'd lived through open-heart surgery and childhood abuse, and now, a widow, she was trying to build a new life for herself.

She was still wounded, though. Life with Dad, she admitted, was never easy. She told me he would look down on her when she showed the slightest bit of emotion or weakness, and could be, at times, incredibly cold. "He was very much of the old guard," Nancy said. "Men didn't cry. Men didn't tell you they loved you. Men didn't talk about what was wrong. It was that Marines mindset, that old way where you were either tough or you were weak."

I asked her what had changed in those final years where he'd softened and had been, for him anyway, affectionate. She said he must have known his days were numbered, and she'd noticed the change when he'd started spending time with me, and then when he began buying gifts for the family.

Remembering those gifts, she recalled a story she'd begun telling around the time my father was first hospitalized: "He told me once that when he was really young he'd give all his toys to his friends because he wanted them to like him. He'd get in trouble for that."

According to Nancy, Dad had been a lot like me as a boy. Sensitive. Soft.

So, how did the soft boy turn into the hard-ass dad I'd known the first twenty years of my life?

"His dad," she explained. "Your grandpa. He got rid of all that in a hurry."

When we were done talking, Nancy showed me her new home and then her new partner Lonnie's garage, where he worked on one of his many fish tanks he was obviously very proud of. With its limitless clutter, his garage was reminiscent of the mess Nancy had had to clean up after Dad died. Strangely enough, that wasn't where the similarities ended: from the right angle Lonnie resembled my dad if he had grown his hair out and worn it in a ponytail.

"How's it going, young man?" he asked, and I told him just fine. "You see that sign out front? He's gonna be the best president ever."

The heat got to us and soon we were back in the house, where Nancy, my stepsister, my stepbrother, and Lonnie's son stood around the tiny kitchen. The women and I talked about who'd gotten divorced, who'd died, and how brutal the summer had been while my stepbrother and Lonnie's son got to talking guns. A little while later my stepbrother ran back to his place to fetch a new pistol he'd bought, which he and Lonnie's son passed back and forth and took apart as the women and I continued catching up. Back home it was nothing for someone to produce a weapon out of nowhere and fiddle with it as if nothing were out of the ordinary.

When I finally said goodbye, Nancy led me back out the front door.

"Your dad was proud of you." She told me this as we stood out in the front yard, both of us sweating and trying not to cry. "He came from a time where you couldn't tell people that, but I know he was proud."

I thanked her for that, and for the talk, and she told me she'd be happy to continue anytime I wanted, about anything at all, whether it was just the weather or my dad.

"He was one of a kind," she said. "Definitely of that old guard."

———

My parents met in 1969 when my mom, Patti Burk, was seventeen years old and carhopping at Tony's Drive-In in Linton. Formerly the Dog n Suds, Tony's was a small restaurant that could handle fifteen to twenty vehicles and sat on a long, rectangular lot where the Veterans of Foreign Wars (VFW) stands now at the end of Main Street. While the Rolling Stones and the Beatles, her favorite, piped out of the restaurant's speakers, Mom hustled trays of burgers and fries to customers waiting in their cars.

The job meant Mom could earn a few bucks and a degree of independence from her overbearing mother, as well as escape her impoverished household. She enjoyed the work, liked getting to talk to all the people she served, but it wasn't without its unhappy moments, like the time a carful of young men pulled a gun on her and tried to make her "go for a ride." Somehow Mom fought her way free and scurried into the main building, where the owner screamed for his employees to get on the floor while he called the police. Mom later testified against the boy, but the result was less than satisfactory: instead of jail time, the young man had been handed another gun and sent to fight in the Vietnam War.

The specter of war in Southeast Asia loomed heavy over young men in town. They had a miserable choice between enlisting or waiting to be drafted. Dad volunteered, and when he met my mother at Tony's Drive-In he was sporting the short-sleeved khaki button-up and green slacks of the United States Marine Corps.

"If I come back here," he'd asked, "will you talk to me?"

For the rest of his week of leave they saw each other at the drive-in, and before Dad left to complete his training in San Diego he'd proposed. Mom told him she'd consider it, and when he returned to Camp Pendleton he wrote and called regularly. Quickly their conversations turned to Vietnam and my dad's increasing doubts as to whether he wanted to go and fight.

Dad's doubts devolved into out-and-out dread. He'd beg my mom to get him a hardship discharge and by then she was so in love she would have done anything. She wrote the necessary letters and made the necessary calls, and before the year was out Dad had received his discharge and returned home to Indiana.

By January they'd both been hired on at the RCA plant in Bloomington, where they worked the line constructing television sets. According to them both, they lived a happy life together in those first few years. They didn't have much in the way of money but they were in love. There were fishing trips, movies, days spent in the sand on Myrtle Beach. Albums' worth of photographs show a young couple crazy about each other. In them, they're always close, my mom leaning into my dad's shoulder, a grin on his face like he'd won the lottery. There are books full of their impromptu trips, pictures of her holding his waist as he drives his motorcycle through the Rocky Mountains and the lush Floridian landscape.

"We were perfect for ten years," my mom still maintains to this day.

The only sticking point was her inability to have a baby. Dad had talked for years about wanting one, preferably a boy, and one doctor after another had told Mom she was incapable. She did everything she could—she saw every doctor, prayed, even gave money to Pat Robertson's *700 Club*. Then, in 1981, she finally became pregnant.

Almost immediately, things fell apart.

The stories of my parents' divorce are predictably unpleasant. Even thirty-six years later my mom holds an incredible grudge against the man who broke her heart. Before he died my dad told me he'd never gotten over her and lived with terrible regret. Mom is still more than happy to go blow-by-blow over what went wrong, and Dad, when he finally opened up, sounded like he'd spent decades rehashing his mistakes.

Back then my dad was hired to make false teeth at an office in town and struck up a friendship with his boss, a dentist who liked to party. They drank heavily, smoked a ton of pot, and dated the female employees. One of them, a young assistant, became my dad's girlfriend, and soon he was spending more time running around with her than home with my pregnant mother.

"I wouldn't know where he was," my mom remembered. "I'd call the office and they'd say, 'Oh, John's out doing this,' or 'John's out doing that,' and he'd be with her. I was so naïve ... if he told me the sky was green I would've believed him."

She never questioned where he was going late at night or why he suddenly cared so much about his appearance. She said his personality changed as he became secretive and started abusing drugs.

When I was born on October 7, 1981, Dad was nowhere to be found. He arrived later at the hospital and kissed my mom on the forehead. "You look beautiful," he told her. "If I had any money I'd buy you a dozen roses."

Dad couldn't afford flowers because that afternoon, while Mom was giving birth, he'd been out shopping for microwaves with his girlfriend. He'd spent the last of his paycheck, a fact my mom discovered months later when she found a receipt with the date in his sock drawer.

The dissolution of my parents' marriage was an ugly affair. Mom still remembers my dad's near-constant harassment that turned to stalking and threats of violence. He'd call at all hours of the night, tell her she belonged to him, and then she'd wake up in her pitch-black bedroom and find him a few inches from her face, his breath reeking of alcohol as he promised he'd rather kill her than lose her to someone else.

Even by my dad's admittance he spiraled out of control. He drank heavily, abused drugs, and ran himself so thin he could barely remember that period in his life. When he talked about those years it was "trying to keep a grip" only to "watch everything fall apart." The life he'd had, the relationship that meant the most to him, had come unraveled, and he just couldn't wrap his head around losing everything.

"I just looked around," he'd told me, "and life didn't look like the one I thought I should've had."

Drinking nearly cost him his livelihood. He'd earned another job, this one in Terre Haute, and on his lunch break he'd drink a thermos of margaritas or beer and fall asleep in his truck. Every day became another opportunity to ruin his life, as he'd drive the forty-five mile commute stone-cold drunk, a risk that could've killed him or any number of people.

"Your dad could be an idiot," Nancy remembers. "Honest to god, he just wanted to die."

That death wish nearly came true. Several times Dad called my mom to tell her he was going to kill himself if she didn't give him another chance, and Nancy said she knew of at least one time where he'd carried a rifle down to the railroad tracks over by where Tony's Drive-In had been and nearly pulled the trigger.

"I just remember," my dad told me, thinking about those dark times, "waking up one day and thinking, how in the hell did I get here?"

———

The same year I was born, psychologist Dr. Joseph Pleck released *The Myth of Masculinity*, a book that presented what he called "the Gender Role Strain Paradigm," and upended a half century's worth of theory about gender. It argues that because gender roles are social constructs and thus impossible to fulfill, the inevitable failure to live up to them can result in psychological damage.

Or, as Dr. Ronald F. Levant and Dr. William S. Pollack argue in an essay in their book *A New Psychology of Men*, Pleck's paradigm "proposes that contemporary gender roles are contradictory and inconsistent; that the proportion of persons who violate gender roles is high; that violation of gender roles leads to condemnation and negative psychological consequences; that actual or imagined violation of gender roles leads people to overconform to them; that violating gender roles has more severe consequences for males than for females." Levant and Pollack then took Pleck's paradigm a step further and focused on what they called "discrepancy strain," which is their term for when males fail to live up to the impractical expectations of masculinity.

In order to view my father's actions, and certainly those of the other men in this book, through the lens of Pleck's paradigm and Levant and Pollack's strain, it's necessary first to acknowledge their problematic nature. For years my father mistreated, abused, and harassed my mother. This is a fact that I've wrestled with for years, and I know, without a doubt, it's left my mother with psychological trauma. No examination is meant to excuse that behavior. These were the actions of a grown man who knew better and should have behaved better—my father admitted as much in our discussions— but it is important, I think, to consider, for the health and benefit of women like my mother and the millions of other women who have suffered abuse, just what kind of forces influence abusive actors like my father.

To get better, we need to study the problem, come to grips with it, diagnose it, and work to solve it. Nothing less than the future depends on us doing so.

In our conversations, Dad was never eager to talk about the beginnings of his relationship with my mom, particularly the circumstances surrounding their initial meeting or the months following. Only once, in all of our talks, did he tell me why that was, and I think it's incredibly appropriate that when he did he happened to be wearing one of his favorite hats that featured the seal of the Marine Corps.

For as long as I had known him, my father spoke proudly about being a veteran, a status that came with an asterisk he never divulged. Though he spent time in a wing of the armed services during a war, the discharge he sought so vigorously casts a considerable shadow over his service. That avoidance of battle hounded my dad for the rest of his life, and his portrayal as a hard-ass Marine was obviously an effort to overcompensate for what he saw as a personal failure.

Dad dropped out of high school to join the Corps, a move he'd tell me later was to both please his father and fulfill his duty as a man like others had done in World War II. He likened it to the call to fight fascism that'd been answered by his father's generation. Vietnam, of course, was a different kind of conflict, a departure from the previous generation's war, which enjoyed widespread support. The reasoning behind this war was suspect at best, and that ambiguity, paired with the brutal nature of guerrilla warfare, added up to an unpopular fight that many young men simply wanted no part of.

My father's diminishing desire to serve in Vietnam mirrored the country's growing doubt. According to a Gallup Poll in 1965, 61 percent of respondents believed America should have sent troops to Vietnam; four years later that sentiment had drastically flipped: Gallup reported in 1969, as my father was preparing to go fight, that 58 percent believed the war to be a mistake.*

History has proven the Vietnam War as one of the most divisive and costly mistakes in American history. Estimates put the economic cost at roughly $160 billion—the equivalent of just under $1 trillion now—and nearly sixty thousand Americans were killed in action.† More than a hundred and fifty thousand were injured, anywhere from seventy thousand to three hundred thousand veterans of the war have committed suicide, and nearly seven hundred thousand suffer from psychological damage.

Politicians and historians have argued the war was a turning point in American history, citing its controversial beginnings, questionable motives, and the atrocities committed against the

---

* Lydia Saad, "Gallup Vault: Hawks vs. Doves on Vietnam," *Gallup*, May 24, 2016, news.gallup.com/vault/191828/gallup-vault-hawks-doves-vietnam.aspx.
† Alan Rohn, "How Much Did the Vietnam War Cost?" TheVietnamWar .info, January 22, 2014, thevietnamwar.info/how-much-vietnam-war-cost.

Vietnamese people. Undoubtedly this compromised the country's standing in the world, as well as damaged its image as an undefeatable superpower. These are some of the obvious consequences, but it's crucial to note the war furthered the divide between men of the Greatest Generation and the Baby Boomers, including men like my father who were torn between fulfilling their duty to their country and protecting their own well-being.

It didn't help that 1968, the previous year, was the bloodiest of the conflict. With escalating warfare and the Tet Offensive, 16,899 Americans died in 1968. My father saw the writing on the wall, telling my mother he had no doubt he'd die if he went to Vietnam, but, again, the men of my father's generation were stuck between the pull of duty and the push for self-preservation.

When my dad talked about his reasons for ruining their marriage, the word he used the most was "shame," primarily for feeling unsure as to whether he could provide for a newborn, the need for my mother to continue working on an assembly line while pregnant, and his shame for having been a coward in the face of fighting in Vietnam. These failures to fulfill the roles of breadwinner and steadfast warrior wreaked a psychological toll on my father and contributed to his breakdown in 1981, a fact he would confirm years later.

Of course, this doesn't explain his behavior in full. Men, particularly white men, in America have enjoyed unbelievable privilege, and when that privilege is threatened their response is to often react violently and in anger. My father's breakdown led to the dissolution of my parents' relationship, but when my mother's reaction was to end the marriage, that privilege, and my father's belief that he essentially "owned" her due to his status as a man, led to harassment. The more my mom denied him, and denied that inherent privilege, the worse it got.

So why did my father ruin his marriage? What was it that led him to seek someone else?

After three decades of introspection, what my dad offered was this: "I just wanted someone who didn't really know who I was."

In my mother, my father had a partner well acquainted with his failings. She'd helped him escape the duty of fighting in a war. That decision to avoid serving is tantamount to cowardice from a traditionally masculine viewpoint, and the day-to-day "indignities" that men suffer from having their partners and loved ones see them fail take a toll. Not to mention their status as a dual-income household provided a new source of role strain.

Studies have overwhelmingly shown that relationships are affected by income, including one published in 2013 by the University of Chicago Booth School of Business that showed heterosexual marriages are more likely to end in divorce once the wife begins to earn more than her husband.[*] This is important to remember, especially as Baby Boomers were getting married just as the American economy welcomed women into the workforce at previously unseen numbers. From 1950 to 2000, the United States Bureau of Labor Statistics reported that the number of women in the workforce increased by over 250 times their postwar levels, a fact that is nothing less than a cultural revolution.

Dad talked at length about his embarrassment at not being more successful when my mother got pregnant. Having dropped out of school to join the military, and living in an economy that necessitated at least a high school education, Dad wasn't guaranteed an occupation that paid sufficiently to cement his status as

---

[*] Marianne Bertrand, Emir Kamenica, and Jessica Pan, "Gender Identity and Relative Income within Households," *Quarterly Journal of Economics*, May 2013, faculty.chicagobooth.edu/emir.kamenica/documents/identity.pdf.

breadwinner of the family. My mom was an early feminist at heart and didn't mind working, but societal and gender expectations are heavy burdens to shake. Studies since that time have shown that women who make more than their husbands actually take on *more* of the household chores, a startling fact that hints that they might be over-performing their gendered roles as to not threaten men's fragile egos.*

"It wasn't like it used to be," Dad said, talking about the economy that necessitated the two of them working full-time jobs. "Used to be that the man brought home the bacon and the woman fried it."

Though painfully antiquated, that expression certainly summed up the changing paradigm of how America functioned. Even though studies show that being the primary breadwinner is actually detrimental to men,† changing technologies that lessened the workload inside the home and allowed women a sliver of independence affected men's status, a status that had provided them their self-worth, and gave way to a new economy where women worked as well. As a result, men needed to find their validation elsewhere.

When my mother ended the marriage, this was yet another blow to my father's brittle masculinity. Because of her job she was able to assert her independence from him, something women have struggled to do in instances of financial dependence, and reject his

---

* Yasemin Besin-Cassino and Dan Cassino, "Division of House Chores and the Curious Case of Cooking: The Effects of Earning Inequality on House Chores among Dual-Earner Couples," *AboutGender*, vol. 3, issue 6, 2014.

† "Being the Breadwinner Is Bad for Men's Psychological Well-Being and Health," *American Sociological Association*, August 2016, www.asanet.org/press-center/press-releases/being-primary-breadwinner-bad-mens-psychological-well-being-and-health.

inherent privilege. My mother's rejection shattered his entitlement, and as is the case with so many insecure men, this rejection shattered his world.

Indeed, a woman standing up to her husband and demanding a divorce was a relatively new development. In the past women were reliant on their husbands financially, and social expectations meant a divorcée would be treated as a pariah. By 1981, however, that had changed dramatically. Though divorce rates had spiked postwar, they had fallen noticeably until they began to rise in the 1970s and peaked for an all-time high in the 1980s, when many Baby Boomers walked away from their marriages.* Again, the privilege and power of men was being questioned in new and unpredictable ways as a woman didn't necessarily need their economic protection anymore, but, ironically and tragically, it meant they might need physical protection from the men themselves.

---

* Ana Swanson, "144 Years of Marriage and Divorce in the United States, in One Chart," *Washington Post*, June 23, 2015.

3

A round four in the morning my mother woke with the distinct feeling she'd been dreaming. Since the divorce two
years earlier my father had been a regular in those dreams,
some of them odd little memories of how things had been—a dinner, holding hands while watching television, the night they'd met
at the drive-in restaurant—and others where he'd made good on
his late-night promises to hurt her. This seemed like a bad one as
he was standing over the bed they'd shared, staring at her as if he'd
never hated anything more.

She blinked away her sleep and realized she wasn't dreaming.
She thought she should've been more surprised to find her ex-
husband lording over her, but it'd become a regular occurrence over
the last few months. Just the week before he'd strolled in the front
door like his name was still on the mortgage. She'd been carrying a
cup of instant coffee into the living room when the bathroom door

opened and there he was, zipping up his fly and asking if she was ready to give him another chance.

"John?" she asked, beyond confused.

He inhaled deeply and seemed to consider his next words. She could smell the bar on him. His shirt was tucked in except for a handful escaping from the waistband of his jeans. His hair, which he had always combed and styled vainly, was mussed as if he had stumbled home from last call and fallen into bed before realizing he needed to get something off his chest.

When he spoke it was with the voice of a stranger. Desperate and violent. He slurred that if she wouldn't be with him she wasn't going to be with anyone. That after he'd killed her he was going into the next room over to kill me. Then he'd move onto my mom's family until there weren't any of us left.

Shaking, my mom said, "John, you need to get the fuck out of this house."

It was the strangest thing how these spells, these moments of murderous rage, could just sweep away like steely clouds on a dreary afternoon. The desire to murder left him and, suddenly, there he was, the boy she'd fallen in love with at seventeen. The change was instantaneous, like a few months earlier when he'd called and threatened to run her off the road and then, when she'd told him she was hanging up, he'd said sheepishly, "I love you, goodbye," as if the marital affections still lingered somewhere beneath his rage.

He turned on his heels and trudged heavily down the hall to let himself out, quietly closing the door behind him like an apology. Mom stayed in bed, under the covers, until she was sure he was gone. For nearly an hour she waited for him to come back, this time with a gun or a knife.

Finally the dark night sky slipped into the bruise-colored dawn. She took that as a sign Dad wasn't going to kill us that day, but he'd be back, maybe even the next night, so she got out of bed on unsteady legs and went into the kitchen for the garbage bags kept under the sink. She pulled out a half dozen and got to work filling them from her closet and dresser. When she was done she snuck into my room and filled one with clothes and another with toys. Having packed enough for a few days, she woke me up and carried me into the living room, her other hand dragging two heavy garbage bags on the verge of tearing. She put a pair of shoes on my feet, zipped up my winter coat, and sat me in the car while she went back for the rest.

At my grandparents' house she made a bed for me on the couch. A pillow from Grandma's bed and a red and blue flannel blanket. The living room was dark except for the TV in the corner that played *AgDay*, the morning show for farmers and chronic early risers. My grandparents had already eaten breakfast, and so the kitchen table was covered in plates slathered in bacon grease and nearly full ashtrays.

"You're staying here," my grandpa said matter-of-factly. "That's the end of it."

"All I have to say," Grandma said, "is if he thinks he can do somethin' to me I'd like to see him fuckin' try."

"Mom," Grandpa said.

"Well," she said, "I mean it. Fuck him and the horse he rode in on."

"I don't know how long we'll stay," Mom said between nervous drags of a cigarette. "I hope not long."

"Damn it," Grandpa snapped, "you're staying here. That's all there is to it."

———

For Mom, living back at her parents' house was bittersweet. My grandma was relentless in her criticisms, and, as a result, her influence grew over me by the day. The independence Mom had gained by marrying my dad all but disappeared; her failures and shortcomings were constant topics of conversation. But at least she felt less vulnerable, less endangered. Dad wasn't likely to break into my grandparents' house, especially considering Grandpa had a shotgun he was known to bust out if he didn't like the looks of someone at the door.

But that didn't mean the harassment stopped. Dad still called and threatened us at all hours of the night. Not long after we'd moved in with Grandma and Grandpa he'd trailed Mom into an office in town and told her, as they climbed down into the building's basement, he was so angry with her he wanted to push her down the stairs. Everywhere she turned my dad was there, whether it was in Bloomington, where she'd be dancing at a bar with a friend only to have him grab her by the arm and order her to go home, or outside my grandparents' house, where he'd screamed at her to quit bleaching her hair.

The breaking point came one weekend afternoon when we were out in the front yard, my mom smoking on the porch while I pedaled my bike on the sidewalk. My dad came speeding down the lazy street and whipped his car into the driveway. High off his ass, Dad got out of the car, all the while telling my mom she was an unfit mother.

Before she could get to her feet my dad had yanked me off my trike and started dragging me to the car. Once Mom saw that he intended to drive off with me, she sprinted across the yard after him. Dad let go of me and sought safety by locking his door and rolling up the window, but Mom wasn't going to let him go so easily. She flung herself up on the Chevy's hood and in that moment she let go of all the pissed-off she'd been building, all the anger from his harassment and threats, and beat the hood until it dented. She would've kept up the assault had my grandpa not run outside and pulled her off.

"You just stay where you are," Grandpa told my dad, "the goddamn cops are comin'."

The police weren't far behind. They told my dad he wasn't to try any more kidnapping attempts and warned Mom to lay off damaging vehicles. In what would become an ongoing trend, they treated my mother's concerns with little care and ignored her abuse. When it was all said and done, my parents again went their separate ways, my dad motoring down H Street and my mom back inside to the safety of her parents' home.

———

One hot summer night my aunt Theiannia invited my mom out for drinks and to spend some quality time complaining about their overbearing mother. Along with Theiannia's husband, Bert, they landed at the Moose to listen to a band and have a dance or two.

The Moose is a squat beige building on South Main Street in Linton that sits across from the post office, a place where members of Lodge 1434 can hoist a few beers and play an occasional hand of poker. That night the lights were low and the band was set up on one end of the main room, a few tables on the other. That's where Mom was nursing a beer when a familiar-looking man sauntered over and asked her to dance.

My future stepdad John had grown up just a block down from

Mom and the two of them went to high school together. Even though they'd never really talked much, he looked like he'd done okay for himself. Dressed in a clean work shirt and jeans, a halfway decent pair of boots on his feet, he was handsome in a rugged way, and it didn't hurt either that Mom had been waiting all night for someone to ask.

Between dances they drank and caught up. John told her he was also newly divorced and with a son back at his house in Owensville. Nearly everything he said drove the point home that he was, first and foremost, a family man.

Within a month he'd asked her to marry him, promising to make a good husband and an even better stepdad. Mom blanched at his initial proposal, but wouldn't go so far as to break things off.

In September he talked her into driving the hour and a half down to Owensville and spending a weekend at his house. He picked her up from my grandparents' and they coasted down US 41, my mom spending the drive deliberating whether she wanted to end the relationship or commit. The home was a small, three-bedroom affair that still had the touches of the woman who'd been there before. John's ex had painted the kitchen peach and hung matching curtains in the windows. The linoleum in the bathroom was cream with pink roses. Mom wasn't impressed, but as she cooked supper for him that night she felt every one of the seventy miles that separated her from life back in Linton.

John didn't talk much, but it was a welcome relief from my grandma's near-constant criticism. Mom tried to get him to open up about his failed marriage with little to no success. He didn't care for small talk and ate most of his dinner in silence. When it was over he left her to scrub the pots and dishes and went outside to tend to his kennel of hunting dogs.

Mom was at the sink when he came back in and shucked off his coat. He approached her as she dried a plate and asked, plainly and with little in the way of romance, "Why don't we just get married?"

Even though they'd been dating for only a couple of months, Owensville seemed like her only ticket out of Linton, her only chance to escape her overbearing mother and my dangerous, unpredictable father.

She'd run out of reasons to say no.

Before things got really bad, John told Mom after she'd quit her job in Linton that he wouldn't hear of her getting another one, that a woman's place was taking care of the house and the kids, and that he expected things to be clean and for dinner to be waiting on the table when he came home from work.

Mom had always been an independent woman, but she looked forward to the possibility of spending more time with me. My grandmother had interfered in our relationship and now Mom wanted the opportunity to repair some of the damage, even if that meant leaving her family behind and marrying a near stranger.

"John and I didn't really talk," she explained. "Getting him to tell me about his life was like pulling teeth. All I knew was that his dad was mean, that he was real into 'discipline.' That's all he ever talked about. 'Discipline this, discipline that.' And maybe I should've picked up on that, but I just wanted a new start."

That new start didn't last very long. One day Mom was wiping down the counters, making sure to keep the house clean, when

John approached her, told her she was doing it wrong, and hit her across the face. She fell onto the floor and watched in disbelief as he pulled out a white handkerchief and showed her how he wanted the sink polished.

"We left then," she told me. "That was the first of nine times we left. We came back eight times, but we left nine."

When I asked why we came back, Mom explained how John had purposefully made her dependent on him. Having her quit her job left her without any source of income. He'd sold off all of her belongings from her life before him and gave her no access to his bank account or paychecks. If Mom wanted to go to the store and buy groceries, she had to ask him for money. She recalled one incident where he'd been sleeping after a late shift and she'd gone to the bank to cash a check for food and when he'd woken up and discovered what she'd done, he dragged her back to the bank and made her apologize.

"The teller just looked at me," she remembered, laughing. "She said, 'Sir, she's your wife, that's normal,' and he just stomped around and said I'd committed a crime. It was craziness."

Making the situation worse, Mom had lost her support net in her family. The move to Owensville meant virtual isolation and my grandmother held the distance against her. The only family member who came to the wedding was her sister Theiannia. Like many abusers, John went out of his way to insulate my mother by purposefully driving a wedge between her and her family, and whenever she questioned his treatment he called her crazy and even went so far as to set up a "mental health checkup" call from his work, which resulted in a phone call where a therapist reported to my mother that John had been telling people she had emotional problems and was lying about what was going on at home.

This left her anxious and depressed for the entirety of our two years in Owensville. She'd suffer abuse as John would regularly grab her, shake her, strike her, throw her against the walls, choke her, and then tell her there was nothing wrong with it, that she was overreacting and "being emotional" or "unreasonable." To lower her self-esteem, John often told my mother she was beautiful, but not as beautiful as his ex-wife.

Abuse became a regular part of our lives. I remember feeling sick every single day when I'd hear John walking in the door because it was only a matter of chance whether he'd be in a good mood or ready to beat the hell out of us. Mom, my stepbrother, and I all suffered. If Mom didn't have supper ready, or if she'd "spoiled" my stepbrother or me in some way, John would lay into her right there in front of us. And if either of us caused a problem, it was our turn.

And the worst thing we could do was "act like a girl."

This high crime consisted of showing even the slightest hint of emotion. If I cried, if I complained, I could expect to be whipped or beaten. I was a sickly kid at that point, a sufferer of severe asthma who could have a life-threatening attack at a moment's notice. John hated that weakness, and he punished my mom and me for it.

Those days were colored by a stark contrast between the hours he was at work and when he'd come home. In the morning and afternoon Mom and I would color and draw at the table in the kitchen, go for walks around the neighborhood, play in the backyard, or else spend time at the library downtown. She'd urge me to use my imagination and encourage my emotions and empathy. Then, after he'd clocked out, John would come home and try to undo every bit of that.

"We were never safe," Mom remembered. "Every day was like waking up into a nightmare."

———

In the summer of 2017, Mom and I drove the same route back to Owensville that she'd once taken with John. After taking the exit, I was confronted with a smokestack in the distance that towered over the treetops. I recognized it as the electrical plant where my stepfather had worked, and seeing it there in the distance struck me with a visceral, physical reaction that mirrored how I'd felt whenever I saw John grow angry. I felt small again, vulnerable and terrified.

When we got to Owensville I found it to be like so many towns in southern Indiana. With a population just over a thousand, it looks, in every direction and on every street, like a community that's slowly eroding. Parked on the downtown square, you find yourself wondering what keeps anyone here. There are a few small restaurants, a couple of stores, but not much to speak of otherwise. On a hot summer day, when the air is still and oppressive, it feels like the smallest of breezes could blow the whole town away.

We went downtown to see the library where we'd spent so many afternoons, a big, brick Carnegie building that looks incredibly inviting, but when we tried the front door we found it locked. Circling around the building, there were windows decorated with the theme BUILD A BETTER WORLD. On the sidewalk, large cinder blocks painted to look like Legos dried in the sun on *Sesame Street* mats with pictures of Big Bird and Cookie Monster strewn in paint.

A sign said the building would open in half an hour, so Mom and I paced around and tried to remember a life both of us would rather forget. The only other people on the square were a group of men working on a road crew. Already their cutoff shirts were soaked with sweat, their arms with barbed-wire and Harley Davidson logo tattoos glowing with sunburn. They wore camouflage hats, and the truck they gathered around had a gun rack in the back window and bumper stickers reading HILLARY FOR PRISON and OBAMA: THE QUICKER FUCKER UPPER. When we walked by them on our way to the war memorial on the square, they were jawing about someone, nearly every other word a profanity or homophobic slur. They paused to eye the two of us suspiciously before we passed and then continued talking.

The war memorial is a simple brick structure with names of those men from Montgomery Township who have served in past conflicts, beginning with the Spanish-American War and following all the way through Operation Iraqi Freedom. For such a small place, many have served—by my estimate over a thousand men from Montgomery Township, which now sports a population of just a little over four thousand. Gold plates designate those killed in action, and there are plenty. To commemorate them, at the bottom of the memorial, behind the glass, are brittle white flowers that have long since dried out.

Looking to waste time, we drove in search of the old house. Three decades had left my mom without much in the way of familiarity with Owensville, so we coasted up and down one street after another hoping she'd remember. Finally, after some circling, she said, "That's it. Right there. The one with the red truck. My god, they've really let it go."

There in the driveway, parked under a leaning basketball hoop with a shredded net, was a giant, jacked-up red truck surrounded by a crowd of cars, most of them appearing undriveable. The structure itself was nearly unrecognizable with brown siding and overgrown grass and bushes, but it was most definitely our old house.

We sat in the car staring until a neighbor across the street, a big man sporting a long red beard and wearing what appeared to be a heavy metal band's shirt with a gas mask on the front, came out of his house, stood on the porch, and glared at us. He was angrily stalking out to the road when we decided it'd be best to leave.

Next, we stopped at a church a few blocks away where Mom would often go when things got really bad. That morning, a man was smoothing out some new carpeting on the steps while drinking Mountain Dew and spitting tobacco juice into an old Planters peanut jar. Watching him work, Mom said, "I went and talked to the preacher and he said, 'You know, I don't usually say this, but you need to get a divorce and get out of there.' And John was there with me, and he got so pissed he banged the desk and yelled, 'This is *my* family and this is *my* wife!' Like he owned me."

That was it for the church and for my mom in terms of having any link to the outside world. As long as we lived in Owensville, as long as she lived in the same house with John, she was trapped.

We returned to the library and inside we pretended to browse the books while Mom shook her head and told me how different everything looked. "We had so many good times here," she said, grazing a book with her fingertips. "You and me would come here most every day and everything would feel all right for a few hours."

Downstairs was a new children's reading room with a table where kids could sit, a rug in the middle of the room with the alphabet and a long, rainbow-colored worm wearing a cartoonish smile. Pictures hung on the walls of the boys and girls who came to listen to stories and make arts and crafts. The boys were all dressed in camouflage and shirts with sports mascots, the girls in dresses and neon pink. The girls drew themselves and their friends and their families in loving embraces, the boys focused on trucks and tanks and other weapons of war.

I walked to a shelf labeled FEELINGS and picked out a random book. There were emotions for every letter in the alphabet, including M, which stood for "Mad." On the page a little boy mouse in striped pajamas was being led away from a gumball machine by a bigger daddy mouse who gripped him by the arm as if he'd lost all patience with his son. The drawing reminded me of the days when I'd get yanked around the house whenever John lost his temper. Thirty years later, standing there in that reading room, I felt an aching soreness as I read the page: *Mad is how you feel when you want to scream and shout because you didn't get your way.*

———

Unfortunately, our situation was not all that uncommon. This country has a frightening epidemic of abuse, large and pervasive. The National Coalition Against Domestic Violence (NCADV) reports that more than 10 million people are abused by their partners every year, that one in three women have been abused by a partner, one in five have been severely abused, that every nine seconds a woman is assaulted or beaten, and that domestic violence accounts for 15 percent of the crime within the United States.*

---

* Dr. Jennifer L. Truman and Dr. Rachel Morgan, "Nonfatal Domestic Violence, 2003–2012," United States Department of Justice, www.bjs.gov/content /pub/pdf/ndv0312.pdf.

Even a more conservative study published by the Bureau of Justice Statistics offered that from 2006 to 2015, there were, on average, 1.3 million domestic incidents every year, and, according to that study, only 44 percent of those were reported to police.* Most of these crimes go unreported, and some have gone so far as to call the problem of domestic violence an "iceberg," as much of the problem remains hidden from sight.†

By a wide margin, men account for the vast majority of the abuse, and that is because domestic violence is a means by which the patriarchal hierarchy is enforced. The violence that women suffer at the hands of their partners is most often a result of those men reacting to what they see as challenges to their authority and tests of their dominance.

In Dr. Nancy Nason-Clark and Dr. Barbara Fisher-Townsend's *Men Who Batter*, they argue that causes of abuse "generally fall under the rubric of 'social control of women' and 'males maintaining dominance.'" This behavior, the violence of the act, has its roots in men's past socialization of emotional stoicism and emphasis on violence as a means of communication.

There is also an economic role as, in John's case, the majority of his abuse took place after frustrating shifts at the electrical plant. Again, patriarchal masculinity, as we know it, grew as a means by which men could survive their arduous labor, but it seems that so much of the physical and emotional abuse men perpetrate on their partners has its causes in the stresses they suffer in the workplace

---

* Dr. Brian A. Reaves, "Police Response to Domestic Violence, 2006–2015," United States Department of Justice, www.bjs.gov/content/pub/pdf/prdv0615.pdf.
† Enrique Gracia, "Unreported Cases of Domestic Violence Against Women: Towards an Epidemiology of Social Silence, Tolerance, and Inhibition," *Journal of Epidemiology & Community Health*, June 2004, vol. 58, issue 7.

or with economic uncertainty, a possibility that seems more likely considering research has shown abuse of female partners increases in times of extreme economic duress, such as the Great Depression and more recently the Great Recession.* As patriarchal masculinity dictates, men are to be stoic workers who put in their time at work and never complain about the difficulty of their labor, the indignities they might suffer, or their inability to provide. Inevitably, they turn this anger and frustration on their families and communities.

Whenever I talked with my mother about her brief marriage with John, I couldn't help but ask her over and over again just what they talked about. To my surprise, she couldn't recall a single conversation that didn't have to do with finances, the raising of children, her chores, or her protests over the abuse we suffered at his hands. He was, as some would say, a typical emotionally unavailable man. In essence, he served as a worker, a disciplinarian, and a provider, but had no interest, or perhaps no capacity, for any of the intimacies upon which healthy and functioning relationships depend, a deficiency, unfortunately, many believe is synonymous with being a man.

In our country this is one of the most enduring misconceptions about gender. While preparing this book, I found so many people still relied on that idea, as if the difference between men and women when it came to emoting were some hardwired contrast. But science disagrees with that assertion, as studies have shown that male infants are far more emotional than their female counterparts.† As Dr. Lise Eliot explains in her book

---

* Daniel Schneider, Kristen Harknett, and Sara McLanahan, "Intimate Partner Violence in the Great Recession," *Demography*, April 2016, vol. 53, issue 2.
† Katherine M. Weinberg, Edward Z. Tronick, Jeffrey F. Cohn, and Karen L. Olson, "Gender Differences in Emotional Expressivity and Self-Regulation During Infancy," *Developmental Psychology*, 1999, vol. 35, issue 1.

Pink Brain, Blue Brain, during observation infant boys were actually more emotional than their female peers before gender socialization.

The change in emotional communication, and, in effect, the denial of emotions altogether, comes later as men are socialized by their parents, peers, and society to shun them. What happens, as Dr. Richard M. Eisler argues in Levant and Pollack's *A New Psychology of Men*, is a male existence where boys develop a schema that "encourages them to attack rather than cry when someone hurts or threatens them" and, as Levant has argued, become "emotional strangers" to themselves.

John whipped and beat me when I didn't fulfill my end of the masculine bargain. If I cried, if I complained, if I was sick, or if I simply fell short of his expectations, that's when I received punishment. This is how childhood works for so many men, and John was no different. His father valued "discipline," much as my grandfather, who punished my dad when he was a kid, and beat into John the sense that to be a man was to be unemotional, and that any violation of that expectation was to be met with retribution.

That violence then serves as the acceptable means of communication for men, which is problematic because, as one of the world's foremost experts on violence, Dr. James Gilligan, has maintained, "the emotion of shame is the primary or ultimate cause of all violence." Because men are taught that they should not have emotions, and that any violation should result in violent reprimand, they are caught in a perpetual cycle. They socialize their children with violence, thus perpetuating the violence moving forward. Then, when they suffer inevitable strain due to their inability to hold themselves up to impossible standards, that shame manifests itself in violence.

They are left with only the ability to express themselves through anger and violence because, as Victor J. Seidler writes in *Unreasonable Men: Masculinity and Social Theory*, "a whole range of 'softer' emotions like sadness, tenderness, fear, are often displaced into anger because this can be seen as affirming rather than threatening our masculine identity." With emotions like sadness, tenderness, and fear being gendered, not to mention a whole range of more complicated actions that rely on those baseline emotions' being not only accepted but put into action, like empathy or intimacy, men who practice traditional masculinity are left with little way to express themselves other than to lash out. In fact, a term has been coined to explain the condition: normative male alexithymia.* The argument here is that men have been taught and conditioned so much to hide and deny their feelings that they've actually lost the ability to communicate them, meaning they are more likely to express themselves through anger and violence than words.

Again, this is in no way an excuse for what my stepfather, John, did. If I were to see him in real life now, I'd love nothing more than to beat the living hell out of him. In researching this book, I was reacquainted with an intense hatred I'd held for years, and wanted to find him and seek retribution for what he had done to my mother and me, but it's important to examine the factors that contributed to his behavior in an effort to address these issues in a real and meaningful way because, as long as we raise our boys to believe that

---

* Ronald F. Levant, "Desperately Seeking Language: Understanding, Assessing, and Treating Normative Male Alexithymia," *The New Handbook of Psychotherapy and Counseling with Men: A Comprehensive Guide to Settings, Problems, and Treatment Approaches*, 2001.

emotions are unmasculine, or that they are signs of weakness, and as long as we use violence as a means of enforcement, we're going to continue raising men who abuse their partners and their children, and who often react to economic shame by enacting violence against others.

John was a living embodiment of just how messed up a working-class man could be. He went to a job he hated, suffered indignities he couldn't process psychologically for fear of being less of a man, and then brought home that stress and took it out on his family. In the process, to make up for his own inadequacies, he controlled his wife socially and economically, ensuring that his male privilege and patriarchal entitlement, those saving graces of an untenable masculine system, were still entrenched.

He suffered in silence and then made damn sure those around him suffered as well.

———

We were supposed to go to the zoo. I remember being excited as I sat down on the living room floor and slipped the mask of my nebulizer over my face. My asthma meant I had to take two treatments a day, and I had learned by the age of five how to take the little glass vials of medicine, break off the tips, and pour them into the mask. I'd press the button on the nebulizer, a little tan box, and the motor would hum to life, sending a cloud of medicine into the mask.

I was in a hurry to go on our trip, so when the medicine was finished, and the box made its telltale noise, I yelled that I was done. Like always, John was pissed off about something and he stomped into the living room and screamed at me. I cried, which only made him angrier, and he beat me so hard I still felt it days later.

My mom ran in and pulled him off. He shoved her and as she walked off toward their bedroom, she angrily slapped the cord of a ceiling fan. Something about that set him off, and he chased her down the hallway and into their room, where he threw her on the bed and began choking her.

My stepbrother Chad and I knew that if John ever got too violent with my mom we were supposed to run next door and get our neighbor, who happened to be John's cousin. So that's what we did. We hurried over there, banged on his door, and then led him back to the house, where he had to pry John's hands off my mom's neck and separate them.

That was our last day in Owensville. The house my mom owned with my dad had finally sold and the little money she got meant she wasn't financially dependent on John anymore. Just like years before, she threw together a few bags and we were out in the car and leaving that house behind for good.

We drove to a McDonald's in nearby Princeton, where Mom bought me a Happy Meal and made a call to Linton. The toy in the box was a Berenstain Bears doll. Brother Bear, I think. I liked him so much my mom went back to the counter and paid to get the rest of the family.

Sitting there, playing with the toys as my body still ached from John's beating, I asked her if we were leaving for good. When she told me we were, it was, and remains, one of the happiest moments of my life.

Three decades later we drove to that same McDonald's and sat in the parking lot.

"I don't think I ever felt better," Mom said, looking at the restaurant. "It was like a miracle, getting out of there."

In the distance the electrical plant's smokestack lorded over the horizon, belching smoke into the sky and reminding me of all the pain and fear. Then, I remembered we could leave whenever we wanted.

4

Family get-togethers are still punctuated by stories about my oddness as a kid. These memories usually center around my imagination and curiosity. When I played with my G.I. Joes or Transformers, the characters didn't simply wage war on one another, like when my cousins or friends controlled them. Their relationships grew and changed, their entanglements complicated as if I was creating a soap opera. That difference, I guess, was predicated on the fact that books occupied most of my time, particularly inappropriate ones like Stephen King novels or the volumes my grandma picked up at a yard sale that talked about surgeries, unsolved mysteries, or historical events like the Holocaust.

My strangeness had its roots in the time I spent with my grandparents after we moved back from Owensville. My mom worked two jobs and after she left for the day I'd beg Grandma to teach me while I waited for school to start. She'd have me sit in front of a chalkboard in the living room and lecture me on matters I had no business learning about.

By the time I started kindergarten, I'd already been exposed to trickle-down economics, the history of war, the Great Depression, the differences between and the histories of the Democratic and Republican parties, and—Grandma's favorite topic as a devout evangelical—death and the afterlife.

For her part, Grandma was a gifted educator who'd never had the opportunity to teach. Instead, she'd built bombs for southern Indiana's Naval Surface Warfare Center. Obviously she'd been waiting for someone to show an interest in learning about any of the myriad of topics she'd come across in her reading—a pastime that must have been incredibly lonely, as she was the only member of the family with a love for books—and I was an apt and enthusiastic pupil.

Looking back, I was so eager because my bout with childhood asthma meant, at an early age at least, I'd spent most of my time indoors. When I was still taking multiple treatments a day and leashed by a plastic tube to a machine, I'd grow restless. It didn't help that my mom and grandma were frustratingly protective. In those first few years, I was trapped and ready to learn.

My first day of kindergarten I came home in tears because I hadn't learned to read yet. I wanted to consume the books Grandma was always lecturing from, but I also wanted to be a writer before I'd ever so much as read a single word. To practice, I'd draw characters in my tablets—mostly stick figures and asymmetrical blobs—and then spend hours creating their stories.

Needless to say, I didn't fit in well with the young boys in my class. When I tried to talk to them about Napoleon or Herbert

Hoover's responsibility for the suffering of the poor during the Great Depression, I got in return either blank stares or a punch in the gut.

Their cruelty surprised me the most. After surviving John's violence in Owensville, my mom had gone out of her way to teach me a better means of communication. She prized my sensitivity and let me know it wasn't shameful. She worked hard to repair any of John's influence. Even at that young age I'd recognized that something was terribly wrong with not just him, but the expectation of men to be unemotional unless violent.

At school I saw dozens of miniature Johns. The boys were needlessly unkind and consistently vicious, and they punished the others for any deviation, be it in how they dressed or how they wore their hair. The bullying was intense. Starting about a month into kindergarten I was finding myself in a fight every few days. A small gang of boys spent their recesses targeting and harassing me until I had no choice but to fight back. Even my teacher refused to do anything about it. She reasoned this was "boys being boys," and it was something I had to learn to deal with. And because she and every other teacher I had didn't take bullying seriously, this went on for years.

But it wasn't just bullies who made life miserable; my own friends were unwitting agents of this oppression. From childhood to manhood, men are kept in line by those closest to them, a terrible perversion of friendship and intimacy that keeps boys and men from ever really connecting with one another for fear of emasculation. This can lead to emotional isolation that's as deadly as a smoking habit.* In fact, studies have shown those who are "lonely" have

---

* Judith Shulevitz, "The Lethality of Loneliness," *The New Republic*, May 2013, newrepublic.com/article/113176/science-loneliness-how-isolation-can-kill-you.

a 26 to 32 percent increased chance of premature death, and men who have friendships involving a lack of emotional intimacy are most certainly lonely.* Those relationships are especially dangerous because they're reciprocal—one man, afraid of his own emasculation, staves off intimacy with his friends, thus making sure they remain isolated.

While I was bullied for being different—and poor, which exacerbated the problem—others were picked for any number of "crimes."

There were the awkward boys whose shyness made them easy targets.

The unathletic boys, particularly if they were overweight like I was.

And then there were the boys I once heard a teacher describe as "not quite right," a state of being that, in the 1980s, everyone had a sneaking suspicion about, even if none of us could quite put our fingers on what it was.

These boys would later escape our town and live openly elsewhere as homosexual and bisexual men. As outliers of traditional masculinity they were victims of socialization, a process by which young boys are taught by their cultures and peers the expectations of their gender roles. Sometimes socialization is as simple and easy as a boy being gifted a toy truck at Christmas (as Hilary M. Lips points out in her essay "Female Powerlessness," boys are "given toys that require skill and perseverance to assemble and use while girls are given dolls") or addressing language differ-

---

* Billy Baker, "The Biggest Threat Facing Middle-Age Men Isn't Smoking or Obesity. It's Loneliness," *Boston Globe*, March 9, 2017, www.bostonglobe.com /magazine/2017/03/09/the-biggest-threat-facing-middle-age-men-isn-smoking -obesity-loneliness/k6saC9FnnHQCUbf5mJ8okL/story.html.

ences that focus on physicality for boys and emotions for girls.* But it can also be as sinister as the time a classmate in elementary school threatened to stab me with a pocketknife for "talking like a girl."

Indeed, socialization's purpose is to not only teach gender expectations, but to weed out any "feminine" characteristic, including, but not limited to, sensitivity, curiosity, creativity, weakness, and a desire to communicate past purposes of utility. This system works on the basis of positive and negative reinforcement. Behave as a traditional male and receive entry into the group. Fail and receive physical, emotional, and social abuse until you have no choice but to conform.

In those years I received the most abuse for my passion for learning and trying to talk about subjects the other boys thought were weird, and this negative reinforcement certainly made a difference. I learned to speak less when around other men. By that same token, I had less trouble, and gained most of my friends, when it came to fulfilling the roles expected of me. Eventually I was able to leave my asthma treatments behind and play sports, and surprisingly, I was a pretty good athlete. My performance on the baseball field or basketball court netted me some credit, and when I played well the bullies tended to leave me alone. Then, when I was in the third grade, my odd interests intersected with masculine expectations as Operation Desert Storm began and every boy in my class became obsessed with war. I'd been taught about every major war since the American Revolution, and so my ability to tell stories meant I could impress my classmates with facts and trivia about "guy things" like combat, weapons, and death tolls.

This socialization constitutes the perpetual cycle of how gendered behaviors are passed down through generations. By and large,

---

* Michael J. Carter, "Gender Socialization and Identity Theory," *Social Sciences*, May 2014, www.mdpi.com/2076-0760/3/2/242/htm.

boys are more likely to bully, and masculine traits have been shown as predictors for bullying behaviors.* Statistically, boys who witness violence in their homes, or are abused by their own fathers—the fathers themselves having been abused as boys—perpetuate the reinforcement with their classmates and peers.†

The act is grotesque in practice, but has lasting cultural effects beyond the horrors of abuse. The negative reinforcement in order to weed out perceived feminine characteristics routinely instills misogynistic and homophobic tendencies that impact personal relationships and political beliefs, often for the rest of the men's lives.

In regard to women, the socialization of bullying among men, or the punishment of characteristics perceived to be feminine in nature, lends itself to the continuation of the patriarchal system. If a boy displays even the slightest hint of femininity—even though men feel as much as women do but are taught to bury it or else— he'll be called a "girl" or a "pussy," both of which were among the regular insults I'd hear either on the playground or while playing sports.

It's this threat of being emasculated, the fear of being "no better than a girl," that drives young men, especially as they are being fed the message that women, with all of their emotions and weakness, are the lesser sex. When a boy cries and he's told only girls do that, he hears the message loud and clear: to show emotions is to be like a female, and to be like a female is unacceptable.

---

* Gianluca Gini and Tiziana Pozzoli, "The Role of Masculinity in Children's Bullying," *Sex Roles*, April 2006, vol. 54, issue 7.
† Joel Schwarz, "Violence in the Home Leads to Higher Rates of Childhood Bullying," *UW News*, September 12, 2006, www.washington.edu/news/2006/09 /12/violence-in-the-home-leads-to-higher-rates-of-childhood-bullying.

Unfortunately, this is one of the earliest lessons in masculinity and it starts the first time a boy hurts himself or suffers disappointment. He'll begin to cry and someone, whether it's a father or a mother, will tell him "boys don't cry." The scolding is bad enough in that it tells the boy he's not allowed to show his emotions and that crying, a perfectly natural coping mechanism, is not appropriate and serves to differentiate the sexes.

The inherent message is obvious: boys are stronger and girls are weaker. As a result, the masculine view becomes the default setting by which the world should be viewed and maintained and the feminine is constantly relegated to being considered defective, or outside the rational. And if men possess the only rational view of the world, then how can women ever truly be heard without being summarily dismissed? In this way, the patriarchy has consistently defined the language and reality by which the world is processed, a control that has been challenged more and more as patriarchal language and logic have been deconstructed.

What perpetuates this socialization is the lifelong threat of being emasculated. If a boy isn't a boy then what is he? A girl or a homosexual, the latter of which carries a particular stigma in the masculine world.

As Dr. John Dececco and David Plummer wrote in their 1999 book *One of the Boys: Masculinity, Homophobia, and Modern Manhood*, "boys learn about homophobia before they understand adult sexuality and sexual identity." As early as kindergarten I can remember boys with effeminate characteristics being bullied and tortured, and back then, before I even knew what a homosexual was, I knew to be one would mean everlasting suffering.

Homophobia among young boys is a reaction to misogynistic underpinnings of socialization, and the resulting bullying is particularly nasty because the boys in question are seen as traitors to their gender. Because this trespass is so bad and so threatening, young boys are vicious toward anyone they perceive as homosexual since they could be mistaken for one themselves, a phenomenon that C. J. Pascoe describes as "the Specter of the Fag," the ever-present concern that boys might be labeled as gay and thus expelled as a pariah.

Some might explain away these behaviors as "boys being boys," which is among one of the most dangerous choruses in American life, but the things boys learn in their formative years stay with them. Socialization that demeans young girls and promotes the objectification of women and homophobia—both in an effort to avoid being mistaken as homosexual—lays the groundwork for a patriarchal society in which male privilege perpetuates, women are demeaned and dismissed, and homosexuals are continually threatened.

These are indisputable facts, but maybe they aren't enough to persuade men that bullying and socialization are problematic. After all, they have the world to gain with the patriarchal structure enduring, but if basic empathy and caring about other people isn't enough incentive, it might be good for men to realize socialization is detrimental to them as well.

To begin, men suffer because their socialization places an emphasis on antisocial behavior and precludes them from excelling in our new economy. Some have argued that schools themselves are failing them, such as Peg Tyre in her book *The Trouble with Boys* and critic of feminism Dr. Christina Hoff Sommers, but this worldview is rooted in the idea that gender differences are natural instead of learned. Boys are encouraged to be rowdy, independent, and headstrong, attributes that don't lend themselves to classroom success.

They are held back more than girls and do worse on the whole than girls, particularly if the boys in question are from disadvantaged backgrounds.*

Again, this could be explained away with "boys will be boys," or passed off as the failings of the educational system, which certainly has its own flaws, but research has shown that these gender differences are often the result of boys behaving as they're expected to rather than out of some deep biological drive.

In *Delusions of Gender*, Dr. Cordelia Fine investigates the perceived differences between men and women and the misconceptions that largely drive our society. One of the more interesting sections of her book concerns how, when tested, boys and girls conform to gender expectations because they are "primed" to do so, but when conditions are changed, the results show a completely different story.

For instance, when boys are tested for empathy, a trait that has been considered "feminine," they routinely score poorly in comparison to their female counterparts. But all it takes for boys to buck the expectations is an emphasis on competition that plays upon their gendered need to win contests.

These experiments show that socialization is so powerful, and gender constructs so internalized, that we unconsciously sabotage ourselves. This means that boys, particularly those boys who have been successfully socialized, are less likely to perform in subjects that have been effectively gendered, whether that's in the arena of liberal arts or in important day-to-day tasks like communication. Our new economy prioritizes these skills. Boys

---

* Jeff Guo, "The Serious Reason Boys Do Worse Than Girls," *Washington Post*, January 28, 2016, www.washingtonpost.com/news/wonk/wp/2016/01/28/the -serious-reason-boys-do-worse-than-girls/?utm_term=.9313a2f1ea73.

being raised as if manufacturing is still a viable vocation are being left behind.

We are only speaking economically, though. In addition to negatively shaping the world, this socialization affects the bullied and bullies alike. As Dr. William Coleman, a pediatrics professor at North Carolina's School of Medicine, reported, bullies are more likely to suffer from substance abuse later in life, and similar studies have shown the bullied are no different. The trauma of socialization follows the afflicters and the afflicted for the rest of their lives.

The consequences are substantial. In a 2015 study published in *Archives of Disease in Childhood*, scientists found that being bullied as a child resulted in "poor physical and mental health" and "reduced adaptation to adult roles including forming lasting relationships, integrating into work, and being economically independent." Similarly, victims were at increased risk for "suicidal ideation, attempts, and completed suicides."

In my own experience, the bullying I suffered did tremendous damage. It made me hate school and the idea of learning, and, because both were central to my identity, it made me hate myself. I couldn't understand what it was that everyone disliked about me and soon the only conclusion I could draw was that there was something very wrong with me. As early as six I suffered social anxiety and depression so severe I was contemplating suicide in the first grade.

I hadn't even known what suicide was until a classmate got in my face and said, "You don't even have a dad. You should just go kill yourself."

When I got home I asked my grandma what he'd meant. Always up for an age-inappropriate conversation, she taught me about self-harm, showed me in books where characters poisoned and shot themselves. In the Bible she turned to the story of Judas and read aloud the passages where he hung himself from guilt for betraying Christ.

I felt like a traitor, too, and for a good long while I couldn't stop thinking about the rope and how maybe I deserved a similar fate.

———

Like many single mothers, my mom struggled to be all things. In order to support us, she worked as a waitress in multiple restaurants, often taking two separate shifts in a day. By the time she'd come home at night she'd be exhausted and depressed from the ill treatment from her male customers. All of it was enough to make her swear off dating for a while, especially after the horror that was her previous marriage.

As much as she tried to avoid the mistakes of the past, she found her next husband in the same Moose Lodge she'd met John. She went there on a weekend night to have a drink, and ended up dancing with a man named Randy. Like John, he was handsome, dressed nice in jeans and boots, and wore a dark beard. They shared a couple of beers and listened to the oldies the band played, and Mom, still wary of dating, said good night. Randy stopped her, though.

"What're you doing this weekend?" he asked.

Mom admitted she didn't have plans, but also said she wasn't looking to date anyone.

"I've got a softball game," he told her. "Come out if you don't have anything going on."

Mom left with no intention of watching him play softball, but when the day came she got in her car and drove out to one of the fields in the country. Sitting in the metal bleachers, she watched

Randy shag fly balls in the outfield, and when the final out was posted he chased after Mom as she made her way back to her car.

Obviously delighted, he said, "You came!"

They chatted a bit, and before she left she'd agreed to dinner and a movie. On their dates he was charming and kind, but even so Mom had her guard up. She'd already rushed into two marriages and suffered the consequences.

"All I wanted," she remembers, "was someone easygoing. Whoever that was, wherever it led, that was the main thing I cared about."

They dated seven months before Randy proposed outside Grandma and Grandpa's house. After saying yes, Mom decided it was time I met my future stepdad. His trailer sat on a lot about a half a block away from my grandparents, and we walked over one weekend afternoon. Randy greeted us at the door with a smile.

I'll never forget that trailer, with its floor swimming in old Mountain Dew cans, every surface covered in opened comic books and magazines, empty containers of Skoal chewing tobacco piled up next to a TV covered in a thick layer of dust. Randy wanted us to move in, but Mom wouldn't hear of it. She wanted a house of her own. She wanted a place to raise me.

They found it a few blocks away, a two-bedroom house in need of a lot of attention. Green and yellow carpet snaked from the floor to the ceiling, the floors were so badly warped that things rolled from one end of the room to the other, and instead of proper doors, the bedrooms had swinging saloon doors poorly fashioned out of plywood.

They got it for $20,000.

I was overjoyed to have a dad again as my own was largely out of the picture. In those first few months Randy was exactly what I thought I should have in a father figure. He taught me sports and gave me old articles from *Sports Illustrated* to read. We bought a miniature basketball goal for the carport and I'd go out for hours and pretend to be the superstars in those pages, all the while getting in better shape and growing stronger. On Saturday mornings we'd sit in the living room and watch professional wrestling, the two of us shouting at the wrestlers in the ring to beat their opponents senseless.

It was a change, to be sure, but as a young kid tired of being bullied and excluded, it was a welcome one. As I played baseball and basketball the other boys accepted me more, and having a male role model who taught me the ins and outs of masculine culture made a huge difference.

Very quickly, I discovered the fraternity of masculinity was easy to enter as long as you didn't mind changing everything about yourself and following the tenets mindlessly.

Things unraveled, though, as they so often do.

Randy was a truck driver for a company out of the nearby town of Bloomfield. He'd followed his father's footsteps into the career, and there wasn't a day that passed when he didn't complain loudly about how much he disliked the work and how badly he was treated by his boss and coworkers. In those moments Randy showed a sensitivity that he'd been hiding from us all along. He wasn't performing like the tough man. Behind closed doors, he was vulnerable and delicate.

His frustration with his job grew until he started missing work. He'd wake up in the morning, tell my mom he didn't feel well, and then spend the rest of the day watching TV or playing video games on my Nintendo. Exhausted, Mom would get home from her shifts at the restaurants and find him unwilling to go back to work the next day. When he did go, he'd come home covered in coal dust from one of his many truckloads, and then refuse to take a shower. Sometimes he'd go up to a week without washing.

To accompany these stretches of time, Randy would suffer psychosomatic illnesses. He'd be sick before calling into work and then feel better until it was time to do it all over the next day. Randy suffered terrible depression and anxiety, and like many men he was unable to seek help. The tenets of masculinity preclude men from addressing any number of illnesses, particularly when it comes to mental and emotional difficulties, which, as a result of socialization, are seen as weak and feminine. The stigma is so severe, in fact, that men account for only a third of all therapist visits in the United States.*

Recent studies have shined a light on this incredibly important and misunderstood problem. In November 2016, weeks after Donald Trump was elected president of the United States, a joint study out of Indiana University and Singapore's Nanyang Technological University showed that men who exhibit the traditionally accepted signs of masculinity were "strongly correlated" to poor mental health.† This is in part due to the self-reliance taught by socialization, but also because of just how unhealthy the masculine ideal truly is. These ideas that we champion in society doom us to suffering, not to mention, as Pleck contends, that our inability to live up to those unrealistic expectations creates its own stress.

Because Randy refused to seek help or communicate with my

---

* John T. Vessey and Kenneth I. Howard, "Who Seeks Psychotherapy," *Psychotherapy: Theory, Research, Practice, Training*, 1993, vol. 30, issue 4.

† Y. Joel Wong, Moon-Ho Ringo Ho, Shu-Yi Wang, and I. S. Keino Miller, "Meta-Analyses of the Relationship Between Conformity to Masculine Norms and Mental Health Related Outcomes," *Journal of Counseling Psychology*, 2017, vol. 64, no. 1.

mother regarding his anxiety and depression, he projected his hurt onto us in the form of abuse. As was the case with my first step-father, John, this is too often the result when men are hurting and have no way of expressing that hurt. Even though he was depressed and anxious, Randy expressed his problems by insulting and berating my mother and me instead of turning to us for support.

Early on in the marriage there were loud and violent arguments that would keep me up late into the night. Mom would try to talk to Randy about what was going on with him, about his continued absence at work, about his poor state of mental health, and he'd respond by lashing out at her, calling her a "bitch," and telling her she was stupid. I'd sit in my bedroom with only my plywood saloon door between me and the fighting, and listen as Randy insulted Mom over and over. It reminded me of those years spent with John in Owensville. Being older, I felt like I should protect her, so I'd march in thinking I'd help only for Randy to turn his anger onto me, inevitably reflecting the abuse I was receiving in school.

Much like what my peers were doing, Randy was projecting onto me his own insecurities. Every day was another opportunity for him to fail at what was expected of him as a man. He was supposed to get up, go to work, and never complain, but his mental illness meant that it was too much for him, and so he failed. Instead of addressing the issues, he took his anger and hurt and disappointment and refocused them on his family.

That abuse continued for the rest of the two years we lived with Randy. Eventually, it took a toll and I developed a stomachache that lasted for weeks straight and kept me out of my second-grade classes for nearly a month.

My stomachache kept me in bed for most of every day, and it terrified my mom and grandparents. Mental illness was never something we talked about in our families. In fact, my relatives made fun of "rich people" who liked to sit around in therapists' offices and complain about their problems. They thought something was terribly wrong with me, be it some sort of strange disease or an advanced case of cancer, which led to my grandma giving me several books on the disease to pore over at the age of seven.

I was taken to numerous doctors and given tests and scans. I'd come home from the offices and then sit there in my bedroom clutching my stomach as the pain grew worse and Randy continued yelling at my mom in the other room or, when she'd had her fill, he'd come in to scream at me for being too sick to go to school while he avoided work with the same kind of problem. Eventually, a doctor suggested I see a therapist, and that only made the abuse worse. Randy, his finger in my face, would scream that I was a little "faggot," or a "little girl" who had to go talk to somebody about my precious feelings.

He wasn't the only person who judged me. Other members of my family, my uncles and cousins, treated me like an outcast. They'd talk about my "having problems" or avoid talking to me, as if the problem might spread. One time I heard a male relative tell somebody that I didn't need "a shrink," I needed "a job in a field" or my "ass kicked" so I could have something to cry about.

I was seven years old.

One weekend I went with Mom to get groceries and afterward we just sat in the car outside the store as she held her head in her hands and sobbed. When Mom's crying subsided, she turned to me and asked, "How would you feel if I divorced Randy?"

"Please?" I asked Mom. "Please divorce him?"

A couple of weeks later things boiled over. Randy and Mom had been having a fight over work and he'd been screaming at the two of us about how much he hated us when my little dog Gizzy, a brown and white Pekingese, wandered across his path. Randy reared back and kicked her hard in the ribs, sending her scrambling behind the couch. Mom jumped up, got in Randy's face, and told him to leave.

Randy moved out and predictably my stomachache left with him.

Mom continued working multiple jobs to make ends meet. She didn't have to deal with Randy's abuse anymore, save for a night, a couple of months later, when she went by his new apartment to retrieve a family quilt he'd taken with him. Before she was in the door he was trying to talk her into getting back together.

She made a beeline for the quilt on the other side of the room, but paused when she saw a hunting rifle just a few feet away. Years before, when they were still married, Randy's father had been discovered preparing to kill himself with that very rifle, and Randy's mother had given it to Randy for safekeeping.

Randy broke down and admitted he'd been considering suicide. With nothing left to protect, he confessed to how he'd been suffering, to all the things he'd been holding in over the course of their marriage. Still hurting from years of abuse, my mom gathered up the quilt and left Randy to sort out his problems on his own.

5

There are blessings and curses that come with a life like this. You don't always understand your circumstances. Even while my mom struggled to put food on our table and our church offered charity, I didn't know we were poor. I kind of thought everyone lived with plywood floors, and that everyone's mom cried because she didn't know how she was going to pay the bills.

I was fortunate to have a mother who shielded me from so much, and a grandfather willing to stand in for my dad who, despite living only three blocks away, was still very much absent.

One of the most enduring memories from my childhood is Grandpa helping out with my baseball practices, standing next to home plate, wearing baggy jeans with suspenders and an unbuttoned flannel that exposed his white undershirt and cannonball belly. A bat in one hand, a dusty baseball in the other, a Lucky Strike dangling precariously from his lips.

He came to every game and every practice, and when my coach needed help he'd climb down from the bleachers, hitch up his pants, and pitch in. I always felt immense pride whenever he'd shag fly balls or carry out infield practice, especially when my teammates called him "Coach Burk," including some of those who had previously bullied me for not having a dad.

After we'd bagged up the bats and balls, I'd hop in Grandpa's green Oldsmobile, where he'd light up another Lucky and search the radio for a Cardinals game or old-time country and gospel. On the way back to his and Grandma's house, he'd go play-by-play and tell me, between drags, how I could improve, how to charge ground balls, how to turn a better double play, how to stretch out from first to get the infielders' throws faster. Among his criticisms and suggestions, he'd always find a way to mix in some praise.

Grandpa was different from the other men I knew, those who withheld approval and chose only to communicate when I'd angered or disappointed them. With John, my first stepdad, it'd been physical punishment. With Randy, verbal degradation. My own father seemed to prefer long, awkward silences.

In much the same way my family treated me as an outsider, they did Grandpa as well. It was common knowledge that Grandma ruled the household, and in her actions she carried out the typical masculine expectations my grandpa fell short of. She'd grown up a tomboy in a family of brothers, was even called "Tom" by those closest to her, wore flannels and jeans, kept a workspace in the shed for her tools and projects, and when something needed to be fixed around the house, she was the one who tackled the chore. She was cold and tried to keep a lid on her emotions, while Grandpa tended to tear up and offer a shoulder to cry on.

Sometimes I'd hear my relatives gossip about their swapped gender roles. They didn't know why Grandpa let Grandma walk all over him, why she most embodied the "Man of the Household" while he just sat there as she criticized and mocked him.

When they thought I couldn't hear, they'd compare us.

Grandpa and Jared.

Both so sensitive.

But where they more or less wrote me off, they gave Grandpa the benefit of the doubt. After all, he had earned that much.

———

Norman Rexford Burk was born in 1923 in the tiny unincorporated farming town of Cass, Indiana, a place so small its post office closed its doors in the 1950s. He grew up dreaming that someday he'd make it to the major leagues and play for his beloved St. Louis Cardinals, but when his father died in 1941, my eighteen-year-old grandpa had to provide for his mother and two sisters. With the Depression having ruined the economy, Grandpa had no choice but to join the Civilian Conservation Corps in order to make money to send back home.

As a member of the CCC he traveled to the Pacific Northwest, where he worked on parks and bridges in Washington and Oregon, calling those states the most beautiful places he'd ever seen. When he returned to Indiana, he followed the call of his generation and enrolled in the Army Corps of Engineers, which deployed him to the European Theater to continue building bridges.

Like many veterans of war, Grandpa never liked to talk much about his experiences. I was always told to leave him alone about the subject, but I was a curious kid who wanted to know everything he wasn't supposed to. Eventually Grandpa confided to me that war was every bit as bad as one might expect. In part, I think he told me his stories because he saw me playing with my G.I. Joes, engaging in glorified battles on my video games, and because you could barely turn the TV on and not find some black-and-white movie that portrayed war as something heroic.

Grandpa didn't just relay the horrors of war; he admitted he was terrified during his entire deployment. This was a break from what I had seen in movies and books, where American soldiers were invincible and unflinchingly brave. It was part of the Cold War era's mythology that lifted U.S. forces in the Second World War to legendary status and taught children like myself that the United States of America, in the face of an evil empire, was the unquestionable hero of the world.

Grandpa's stories were more complicated. Instead of iron-jawed warriors, the soldiers at his side were frightened young men who only did the best they could when faced with terrible circumstances.

In his biggest story, the one in which he earned his Purple Heart, Grandpa drew the short straw and had to rush a German machine-gun nest in northern France on November 14, 1944. In our family the story had become the stuff of legend. When others told it, they portrayed Grandpa as if he were John Wayne charging up a hill, the Stars and Stripes waving dramatically against a backdrop of enemy fire as patriotic music swelled.

When Grandpa relayed the story to me it sounded like a twenty-one-year-old young man did as he was ordered and, for his trouble, got shot and a piece of German hand-grenade shrapnel lodged in his eye. It ruined the fantasy for me, and when I asked if he was scared, he surprised me by saying, "That's not the kind of thing you expect to come back from."

———

Of course, with time, we've come to realize the truth Grandpa admitted to me represents the realities of war much more than movies.

We now live in a time where a film like *Saving Private Ryan*, which opens with a shot of Tom Hanks's quaking hand, more embodies the truth of war than any of the old standards. Some might say there's no problem with that mythologizing, but it bears remembering that so much of modern masculinity is built upon the idea that men are supposed to live up to the example of the Greatest Generation, a group whose achievements have been appropriately lionized but whose humanness and frailty have been largely painted over.

Veterans have long been held as idealized American men. In history and popular culture they have been treated like superheroes who fought valiantly to wipe the map free of Nazi Germany. This fabrication serves a purpose. Certainly when considering modern warfare, World War II is the most heroic war, a face-off between good and evil on a global scale, and the version of history Americans have embraced positions our country as not just heroic but *the* hero of that conflict. That popularized view of American soldiers is problematic for the country and the heroes it glorifies.

In the last seventy years we have repeated this mythology, an oversimplification that has had real consequences in the progression of our country's ideals and the way in which we perceive the world. Because soldiers have been upheld as the pinnacle of American masculinity, we have further swallowed the lies of toxic masculinity and its resulting culture of militarism.

It's obvious that our culture's ideal man is a reflection of the soldier. Like those troops in the John Wayne movies my grandpa disliked so much, men are expected to be unrelentingly strong, stoic, and unbreakable. They are to be the pillars upon which society's foundation is built, and their courage and strength are considered the only thing standing between free society and the forces of barbarism.

This worldview means that America must always be ready to

fight. It's important when examining history to remember that men are taught that communication is a weakness, and that the only way a man can express himself is through anger or violence. With that in mind, the wars in Korea, Vietnam, Afghanistan, and Iraq certainly make more sense. Each was an opportunity for America to assert its dominance, and each resulted in massive casualties well after it became obvious that victory in a traditional sense was unachievable.

Culturally, the lie that American veterans were steadfast and daring only fed this narrative of masculinity. If our fathers and grandfathers could survive a depression, ship off to Europe or Asia, and fight against the forces of fascism, then we should be capable of conducting our civilian lives without complaint. This, again, means that men of succeeding generations are faced with living up to expectations they are incapable of fulfilling.

The men who set that example are similarly victims of the false narrative. Like my grandpa, veterans of war often embody the "strong, silent type" persona, or that of the man who sits alone with his thoughts and very seldom communicates the horrors of war he's witnessed. The burden of that solitude is a curse all its own. These men, who have given all for their country, are expected to contain their traumas and remain stronger than their experiences.

It should come as no surprise that our understanding of posttraumatic stress disorder in veterans has evolved parallel to our realization of the hollowness of masculinity. In World War I, sufferers of PTSD were diagnosed with "shell shock" after enduring relentless bombardment from artillery. As traumatized soldiers exhibited panic and fear, it was reasoned that something must be physically wrong, as men would never suffer emotional or psychological damage. The term "shell shock" was invented to give cover, the diagnosis "commotional," or "related to the severe concussive motion of the shaken brain in the soldier's skull."*

Similarly, in World War II, the term "combat fatigue" put the onus on physical maladies while doctors were beginning to understand the psychological implications. Despite popular culture's rendering of them as unshakable heroes, the men of World War II were distinctly human and fell prey to the unthinkable stress of battle. In 1943 alone, the year Grandpa joined the army, 40 percent of all evacuations in the Pacific were "mental" in nature, and over the course of the war nearly 1.4 million soldiers would be treated for combat fatigue.†

Though the military was just beginning to understand the implications of the mental toll of combat, that understanding was certainly not universal. The legendarily gruff Lieutenant General George Patton toured a field hospital in Sicily in 1943 and came across Private Charles Kuhl, who'd been admitted for psychological reasons. An incensed Patton attacked Kuhl, slapping him and demanding he be thrown out of the hospital, as he was a coward. Within days, he'd attack another private named Paul Bennett and release a directive to the Seventh Army ordering them not to admit such men, threatening court martial.

For his actions, Patton would be reprimanded by his superior, General Dwight Eisenhower, and there were calls for him to be relieved of his command. But with time, Patton would be mytholo-

---

* Charles S. Myers, "A Contribution to the Study of Shellshock: Being an Account of Three Cases of Loss of Memory, Vision, Smell, and Taste, Admitted into the Duchess of Westminster's War Hospital, Le Touquet," *The Lancet*, February 1915, vol. 185, issue 4772.

† "The Mental Toll," *Public Broadcasting Service*, 2003, www.pbs.org/perilous fight/psychology/the_mental_toll.

gized into a symbol of the grit and determination of the American male. Movies would be produced, books written, and Patton's problematic treatment of Kuhl and Bennett would be widely regaled as a blow against the "pussification" of culture. In campaign speeches leading up to the 2016 presidential election, Donald Trump would reminisce wistfully about "Old Blood and Guts" and criticize the modern military by saying, "George Patton was one of the roughest guys, he would talk rough to his men . . . we don't have that anymore."*

Patton's rehabilitation was largely a result of the Academy Award–winning movie *Patton*, in which the general was portrayed by George C. Scott as a stern and valiant warrior who proclaimed, "All real Americans love the sting of battle." That movie was released in 1970 as the United States was languishing in Vietnam and longed for the glory years of World War II. Because of that movie, Patton was championed by men like my father, who spoke glowingly about the general, and also Donald Trump, as both men overcompensated their own failures with masculinity—my dad finding his way out of the military before serving and Trump's five deferments that kept him out of the service—by pointing to this figure who would have despised them both for their "cowardice."

This overcompensation, in part, created another divide in the conscience of American men. From that point on there were two military personas men could fall under, that of General Patton or that of Private Kuhl, and men like my father and Trump, who have much to compensate for, were more likely to embrace Patton and

---

* Emily Flitter, "Trump's Obsession with WW2 Generals Strikes Sour Notes with Historians," Reuters, February 2016, www.reuters.com/article/us-usa -election-trump-generals/trumps-obsession-with-ww2-generals-strikes-sour -note-with-historians-idUSKCN0VY2XJ.

his abusive, fascistic tendencies as a means to build up their own flagging masculine identities.

Considering how regularly Americans profess their love of the military, it's worth noting how this overcompensation can routinely lead to service members being left in the lurch, particularly when it comes to treatment and benefits. The astonishing gap between the rhetoric and the depressing reality is sewn into the narrative of masculinity and encapsulated by the rehabilitation of George Patton. Men like Trump and my father, and others who elevate idealized service members as the paradigm of masculinity, are engaged in an active fantasy that both furthers the patriarchal system and creates an environment wherein the veterans being idolized are actually penalized for any failings. Because they are brave, they earn the outward show of respect, but when they are in need of assistance, which "real men" never are, they're quickly forgotten lest the fantasy come crashing down.

Especially in the modern era of continual war, this means our millions of veterans receive substandard support; often, it could be argued, because of the public perception that warriors are invincible. According to a shocking 2013 study by the Institute of Medicine, the Departments of Defense and Veterans Affairs had failed to provide adequate care or services for America's returning veterans, a realization made even more concerning when considering just how much they were in need.* According to that study, 44 percent reported "difficulties," while one in five suffered from PTSD. In addition to a myriad of health issues, including injuries and widespread substance abuse, veterans

---

* Karen McVeigh, "U.S. Veterans Face Inadequate Care After Returning from War," *The Guardian*, March 26, 2013, www.theguardian.com/world/2013/mar/26/us-veterans-inadequate-care-war.

were struggling to return to the workforce as the unemployment rate was nearly double that of the national average.

In September of 2017, the Department of Veterans Affairs released a similarly alarming study that showed the suicide rate among veterans was twenty-two points higher than average and estimates put the number of suicides among veterans as high as twenty a day.*† Some conservative estimates put the rate of drug or alcohol abuse among veterans at roughly 20 percent, with others arguing the rate was much, much higher. But still, even while a crisis among our veterans looms, economic and public support have failed to address the very real need as the myth of masculinity continues to hamper those who aspire to it.

———

My grandfather returned home a decorated war hero, but was haunted by his experiences in Europe. To combat his trauma, Grandpa relied on the only acceptable means for a real man to drown his sorrow: the bottle. Almost immediately he became a heavy alcoholic. He sank his paychecks in beer and poker, often staying up for days in order to drink and play cards.

At a rowdy poker game in Indianapolis he met my grandma. She was married at that time to an older man legendary for his boozing and bad behavior. He was of small stature, and like many

---

* "VA Releases Veteran Suicide Statistics by State," Veterans Administration, September 2017, www.va.gov/opa/pressrel/pressrelease.cfm?id=2951.

† Leo Shane III and Patricia Kime, "New VA Study Finds 20 Veterans Commit Suicide Each Day," *Military Times*, July 7, 2016, www.militarytimes.com/veterans/2016/07/07/new-va-study-finds-20-veterans-commit-suicide-each-day.

men, he overcompensated for his diminutive size; he brawled, was prone to bouts of anger, and terribly mistreated my grandma and their three children. In fact, years later, he'd bet his daughter on a losing poker hand, forcing her to have to escape his house to avoid having to sleep with one of his drunken buddies to pay off his debt.

Grandma left her husband for my grandfather, and they moved to Linton, the town where my grandpa had always dreamed of living. Back then, before the fall of industry, Linton was a growing town that in the surrounding farming communities looked like a thriving metropolis. Grandpa loved to take his new family downtown on a Friday night, park in a lot, and just watch the traffic come and go as people streamed in to catch a movie or grab dinner.

His drinking was such a problem that Grandma would never let him live it down. Until he died she was still criticizing him for his boozing after the war, even though he gave it up when my mom, four years old, walked into his bedroom as he was listening to the Cardinals on his radio, and told him she didn't like it when he drank. After that, he might have had one beer a month during baseball season, but largely let it go.

He got a job in 1962 manufacturing bombs and shells at the Crane naval base, and earned the nickname "Windy Burk" because he liked to talk on the line. At home, he sat with his coffee and cigarettes and mostly nodded as the people around him chatted, the only exceptions being when Grandma went too far or somebody got upset. Though he delegated leadership of the home to her, he was quick to interject if he thought she'd hurt her kids' feelings, especially my mom, his only child. If someone was down, or worried, he'd speak up and reassure them, which was unbelievably rare when it came to men in my family.

In all of my childhood, he was the only man I saw cry unabashedly. Sometimes I'd hear them, through doors and walls, but my grandpa was never ashamed like the rest of them. I'd see the telltale twitch over his eye that he'd earned in the war, and before long there it was. I asked him once if it was okay. For years I'd gotten in trouble anytime I'd dare cry openly. I'd been beaten by John, belittled by Randy, and bullied by the other kids at school. I'd come to think of it as one of the worst things a man could do.

"If you cry, you cry," he'd said, drying his cheek with one of the white handkerchiefs he always kept in his back pocket. This was after Grandma's Aunt Evelyn had come to visit, and suffering from the early effects of Alzheimer's, she'd gotten lost in the house and caused a scene. Grandma's reaction had been to act like nothing was wrong, or that the suffering was "part of life," which was the phrase the men in my family used when talking about anything remotely tragic. Grandpa had been the only one to cry, and of that weeping he'd said, "There's no shame in it."

I'd been confused about masculinity for as long as I could remember, harbored suspicions that something wasn't right, but it was Grandpa's behavior that sealed that distrust. I still felt incredibly alone and shameful about my own shortcomings. Everyone I met, every father figure who entered my life, continually reinforced the notion that I should conduct myself as all of the other men around me, except for my grandfather, who embodied a contradiction so staggering and world-shaking that I couldn't help but reassess what it meant to be a man.

I watched him weep without shame and treat his loved ones with affection and tenderness. When somebody got sick, whether it was my mom or Aunt Theiannia (who would die of cancer when I was sixteen), it was Grandpa who sat next to the bed and watched over them. He would cry and hold their hand, and whisper to them that he loved them and was there for them.

These behaviors, so antithetical to traditional toxic masculinity, would have been rejected in nearly any other man. Undoubtedly my male relatives would have poisoned my view of him and contradicted his influence if he had been anybody else. But Grandpa Burk was a war hero. He'd proven himself in an incontrovertible fashion, and he didn't need to display his Purple Heart or other medals to validate how he conducted his life.

In him, I saw it was possible to be, in many ways, a traditional man while also bucking the unhealthiest tenets of stoicism, coldness, and anger as the only means of communication. Grandpa was fine letting women be strong. He didn't have to pretend to be invulnerable or hide his tears until he was alone in a dark room with only the walls to hear. He'd earned the right to live his life honestly without fear of punishment by the patriarchal world he inhabited, and by blood and by shrapnel he'd earned the right to teach me one of the most valuable lessons I'd ever learn: "If you cry, you cry. There's no shame in it."

6

The first time I met my future stepdad Jon I was nine years old. I was in the living room when he came in the front door, a pizza in one hand, a plastic Walmart bag in the other. He was younger, had long dirty-blond hair, wore a NASCAR shirt with a couple of tattoos peeking out from under the sleeves. While Mom and I got out the paper plates, Jon pulled a mess of wires from the plastic bag and got to work hooking them up to the back of our TV. Within a few minutes he turned to Channel 22, which had always been a storm of static. Now, as we sat down with our pizza, the movie channel Showtime announced that in a few minutes the 1990 live-action version of *Teenage Mutant Ninja Turtles* would begin.

Mom told me to get my TMNT toys, which were buried in the bottom of my shoebox of action figures, and when I came back into the living room she and Jon had disappeared behind a closed bedroom door. Confused, I set up Leonardo, Donatello, Michelangelo,

Raphael, and their assortment of rivals, ate my pizza, and enjoyed my first night of stolen premium TV.

After that, Jon moved in without so much as a discussion. During the day he'd go to work, and then return with another armful of clothes. Mom never told me what was going on, but it was quickly obvious our visitor was no longer a guest. It was good fun, though, which was a relief after John and Randy. All Jon wanted to do was listen to Guns N' Roses and Metallica on the stereo and watch action movies on the VCR. It was like having the best parts of Randy all over again, meaning we got to engage in that typical male bonding without all of the verbal abuse. Every night felt like a party, and that was a damn sight better than what we'd been living with for most of my life.

In some boxes in my mom's closet I found a few of Jon's yearbooks, pictures of him and his friends, a sleek red electric guitar with Jon's fingerprints smudged on the surface. Then, way in the back, I discovered a dark gray welder's mask onto which had been painted in red the words SEX DRUGS AND ROCK N ROLL.

For a long time I stood in that bedroom staring at the mask. I was only nine, but I'd heard about sex. Sure, I didn't know the particulars, and what little I did know had been gleaned from ignorant recess discussions with my idiot friends and what soft-core movies I'd watched on our bootlegged Showtime. Rock 'n' roll made sense, too. It was Axl Rose screaming on "Paradise City." The machine-gun guitars as Metallica's "One" broke down. The Elvis and the Stones that played on the radio in the kitchen as I threw a rubber ball against the back door for hours.

But drugs? All I knew about drugs was my teachers telling me not to use them, the public service announcements on TV showing sizzling eggs as ruined brains, the villainous dealers all the action heroes were shooting up or dragging to justice.

Carefully, I set the mask back where I'd found it and decided I wouldn't say a word.

A few months later, there was a pounding on our front door around six in the morning. Mom was up getting ready for her shift, and I was still tucked in bed. A flood of men rushed into our house and began going through all of our things as my mom stood back and protested and I bawled my eyes out. They went through my clothes, my toys, everything. They demanded to know where Jon was and called Mom a liar when she told them he was already at his shift at the pallet factory.

I tried to ask Mom what was going on, but she didn't want to explain it to me. All I knew was that Jon was in trouble, which I gleaned from the way my grandma kept saying "Oh my lord, oh my lord, oh my lord" whenever Mom brought the subject up at their kitchen table. Grandpa went and bailed Jon out of jail, and he was back in the house that night as we tried to clean up the mess the police had made.

Things were quiet for a while. I knew something was brewing, but nobody would fill me in. It came to a head that summer when we went to the movie theater in town and watched *Terminator 2: Judgment Day*. When we came out of the theater our neighbor Tony, a policeman, was waiting for us. He spoke to Jon while my mom kept me at a distance, and then we drove back home. During that ride Jon was quiet and Mom was upset. When we got there, Jon surrendered himself to the police. He wouldn't return to our house for another three years.

———

Born in 1964, Jon grew up with a stern and distant military father who would eventually reach the rank of first sergeant in the United

States Army. As a kid he'd sit in the stands as his father worked as a stock car mechanic at the Tri-State Speedway in Haubstadt and dream of getting behind the wheel like his NASCAR heroes. On TV he watched the Dallas Cowboys and Evel Knievel jumping his Harley Davidson on *Wide World of Sports*.

When he was sixteen he left home and moved in with a group of older guys who drank and ran around, eventually forming a band called Legend that performed here and there. By that time he was living out his fantasies and embodying the stereotype of the rock 'n' roll star, the outlaw, the rebel without a cause.

This role is a popular one for young men. While it's contradictory in many ways, as rock stars exhibit characteristics contrary to traditional masculinity, what with their artistic expression and their predilection for long hair, makeup, and outlandish costumes, the role is still in line with masculine expectations, especially in regard to self-reliance and emotional stoicism. The outlaw, after all, takes chances with his life in much the same manner as most men in order to flaunt his own safety. Just as Evel Knievel jumped a dozen Greyhound buses as a daredevil with a death wish, young men who fancy themselves outlaws live as if the specter of death doesn't haunt them.

Jon was no different. In his Olds 98, driving down the hilly back road in Linton called White Rose, Jon was speeding so fast that he hit one of the hills and went airborne. Eventually he had to be pulled out of the wreckage and nearly lost his eye.

By a large degree, young men with "macho characteristics" are more dangerous on the highway.* Doubtlessly, everyone has seen

---

* Barbara Krahe and Ilka Fenske, "Predicting Aggressive Driving Behavior: The Role of Macho Personality, Age, and Power of Car," *Aggressive Behavior*, December 2001, vol. 28, issue 1.

this when a young man in a sports or muscle car comes screaming down the interstate, weaving through traffic and endangering themselves, as well as everyone else.

This behavior is very common for young men, and studies have shown a direct link between gendered behavior and dangerous driving, including one experiment published in *Accident Analysis & Prevention* where young men were put into driving simulators and when prompted with "masculine" language began driving more aggressively than when given "feminine" or neutral prompts.* Much like the lack of empathy or social knowledge discussed earlier, this aggressiveness is performative instead of naturally occurring, meaning when a young guy comes racing down the highway, he's doing so in order to show everyone what a strong man he is.

So much of this behavior is wrapped up in men's insecurities, but it also has to do with trying to live up to the image of their fathers and the figures of popular culture that came before them. Jon's father, the stern veteran, presented to him an unflinching role model that he had to try and mimic. Certainly the soldier and the outlaw have much in common in regard to their perceived lack of fear of death: the soldier storms into a cloud of gunfire while the outlaw flirts with death without flinching. Undoubtedly, as Jon raced down White Rose toward his wreck, he must have felt a kinship to his father's courage and his role on the speedway, where drivers pushed themselves further with little regard to their own safety.

It bears repeating that Jon's role models were men who displayed a different type of masculinity, but still inhabited hegemonic masculinity all the same. There were the football players who put their

---

* Marianne Schmid Mast, Monika Sieverding, Michaela Eslen, Karin Graber, Lutz Jäncke, "Masculinity Causes Speeding in Young Men," *Accident Analysis & Prevention*, March 2008, vol. 40, issue 2.

lives on the line with every snap of the ball, but also the daredevils and the rock stars.

Evel Knievel dressed in red, white, and blue jumpsuits, a nod toward Elvis Presley's signature look, but he faced down danger with frightening regularity, all the while pretending he was fearless. The first few lines of his bio page on his website paint a picture of a rough-and-tumble outlaw, detailing how he gained his moniker:

> After a police chase in 1956, in which he crashed his motorcycle, Knievel was taken to jail on a charge of reckless driving. When the night jailer came around to check roll call, he noted Robert Knievel in one cell and William Knofel in another. Knofel was well known as 'Awful Knofel' ('awful' rhyming with 'Knofel') so Knievel began to be referred to as Evel Knievel ('Evel' rhyming with 'Knievel'). He chose this misspelling because of his last name and because he didn't want to be considered 'evil.'
>
> And thus the legend was born . . .*

The story being told here is meant to sound badass. Who wouldn't want to get their nickname following a police chase, a charge of reckless driving, and a conversation with a night jailer? It's too cool. It's too masculine. And certainly Evel's entire career followed a similar trajectory, a badass who broke nearly every bone in his body and later beat a rival with a baseball bat. All along the way, he faced every new challenge undaunted, faced his own demise with a stiff upper lip and an eye toward the next peril.

Part of the problem, besides the influence Knievel had on young men who idolized him and the proliferation of a lifestyle that was self-destructive in numerous ways, was that Evel was largely a

---

* "The Man," EvelKnievel.com, evelknievel.com/the-man.

showman who wore his persona like one of his many flashy jump-suits. Despite his bravado, his character was just that, a character, and despite the legend of being fearless, he was scared when sizing up his jumps. In a late-life interview with *Maxim* he admitted, "I loved the thrill, the money, the whole macho thing. All those things made me Evel Knievel. Sure, I was scared . . . but I beat the hell out of death."

That article lionized Knievel's "drinking, carousing, chasing women," and all his efforts to live up to "his wild-man rep." It's a love letter to the persona and all the surrounding bullshit. Later, as the interview is winding down, after Evel has shown off his .44 Magnum and grabbed a beer, it mentions his son Robbie, the "only member of the family who had the guts to stand up to his irascible father." Evel admits he "admired" his son for that before changing the subject to Robbie's own forays into stunt driving, which he credits Robbie for being better at, but only because "he started earlier, and he has better equipment."

Upon a little scrutiny, Evel Knievel comes off as a real asshole and a pathetic man, which conflicts with the image presented to young men like Jon in the 1970s who watched him soar through the air like a real-life superhero. In media around the world, Knievel was held up as an idol of masculinity. There were lunch boxes, action figures, costumes, and pinball machines, all of them aggrandizing a jerk who broke his bones to stuff his pockets and present himself as a true man.

Reckless behavior isn't just limited to daredevils. Certainly they weren't jumping canyons in makeshift rockets, but the risks rock stars took with their well-being was similar imperilment for similar purposes. Rock stars regularly push the limits of good taste and act contrary to principles of self-preservation in order to flaunt their lack of fear and pad their masculinity. Sure, they occasionally paint their faces, wear lipstick or eyeliner, and appear in gaudy outfits, but those bands and artists who truly exemplify the rock-star ethos are dedicated to following the tenets of manhood, whether that's showing courage in the face of doom, or the perception of women as objects with nothing to offer but sexual gratification.

The rock-star lifestyle, which Jon lived in his early years, is one of flagrant self-abuse. One only has to look at luminaries like Keith Richards, who has made millions off of promoting his rampant drug abuse and the fact that he's survived decades of hard living, and the scores of young men he's inspired. This is tied in with many well-known masculine behaviors, such as binge drinking, drug abuse, and dangerous sexual practices, all of which can start out as performance until the man performing them morphs into the character. Many young men, myself included, have drunk or used drugs in order to show our male peers how tough we are and then suddenly realized we've suffered consequences or developed addictions.

That's not what rock 'n' roll's about, though. Rock 'n' roll is, in many ways, the embodiment of American cool, about knowing there are possible consequences to your actions and yet going ahead undaunted. It feels unbelievably cool to do these things, and any man who tells you different is either in denial or lying. This is why so many of us lay it on with the gas pedal, drink heavily, or turn our music up way too loud. To actively thumb your nose at death, even when you're aware of why you're doing it, is to feel as cool as you possibly can.

When Mom first met Jon they were working at a grocery store called Hanley's in Linton. She didn't really interact with him back then, as he was a young stocker and she worked in the deli, but she remembers him being a partier, a guy who listened to Led Zeppelin and Ozzy Osbourne. The single mother of a kid, she couldn't have seen herself dating someone like him.

Years later, she arrived at the Palace Bar downtown to drink a couple of beers. She told herself she'd stay just long enough to finish her pack of cigarettes and then go home. This was after she divorced Randy, and she needed to get out of the house. Jon came in with a group of his friends and they chatted for a few minutes. He asked if she'd stick around and my mom showed him her nearly empty pack of cigarettes. Jon went and bought her a new pack. The rest is history.

Mom made it clear if they were going to date he'd have to grow up and leave the partying and drugs behind. Jon told her he would, but his past wasn't quite done with him. Before they started dating Jon had been hanging out at the city park with his friends when someone approached him looking to buy LSD. Jon says he told them no over and over, but eventually he gave in and introduced them to a dealer. The buyer was an undercover cop, and Jon was arrested. He was sentenced to three years in prison, meaning we were on our own again.

7

In the summer of 1995, my mom was trying her hardest to keep our life together. Jon was behind bars, leaving her to handle the house and the bills. She worked overtime at her factory job and occasionally we'd go into the plant after hours together and clean the break rooms, offices, and bathrooms for extra money. On the weekends she'd visit Jon, sometimes sneaking hamburgers to him in her bra, sometimes taking me, scared out of my mind, to sit in a cold visitation room to talk to Jon about life in prison.

When we'd visit we'd walk into the caged prison yard while men catcalled my mother from their windows. Every step I took was filled with budding terror. Inside we were patted down, led through metal detectors, and then made to wait for Jon to be fetched from his cell. I knew the men around us were criminals, many of them violent criminals who'd committed terrible crimes. They'd dealt drugs, stolen property, hurt people, assaulted women, and sitting there among them made me feel about as unsafe as I could imagine.

I'd read about prisons, had devoured every book my grandmother kept hidden about murderers and true crime, but being there inside the cold concrete walls only served to make the reality vivid and more frightening.

Inevitably a guard would usher Jon into the room. He'd lost a ton of weight, looked like he'd aged years already, and as he sat there in his blue work shirt and jeans, he'd avoid talking about life behind the walls and focus on our lives outside of them. He'd ask what'd been on TV lately, what we'd been eating for dinner, and when the subject was broached as to how we were doing, my mom would always tell him we were doing just fine.

The truth is, we were working just to survive. I was thirteen, about to enter junior high, and during the day I'd do my part and keep things clean and then help Mom get to work replacing the siding on our house. She was trying so hard to keep herself busy while Jon was in jail that she enrolled in the distance education program at St. Mary's College in Terre Haute and did her home-work between the nightly collect calls and stretching her money for our meals. There was no skirting the issue of our poverty anymore. Times were incredibly lean.

For a brief period, even as we struggled, I felt relief. Somehow we'd gone through hell with John and Randy and come out the other side with each other. Being poor didn't bother me. Even the bullying at school was beginning to lose its sting. I could handle being called names and getting shouldered into my locker if my home was a safe place to lay my head.

That illusion, however, was soon broken.

August 18, 1995, was a Friday, and like every Friday I got my allowance and went straight downtown to the comic book shop on Main Street and sorted through the newest issues of *X-Men* and *Fantastic Four*. I had the routine down, as I could buy two new comics, possibly a couple more from the discount box, and then head across the street to Kohlhouse Video, one of my favorite places in the world, to rent a video game for the weekend. By the time I'd get home my mom would have ordered us a pizza, our one extravagance for the week.

I knew immediately something wasn't right. There were three police cars lined up on our street and our neighbors were milling about on their porches. I asked Mom what was going on and she told me that Pam Foddrill had gone missing.

Pam lived two doors down with her elderly mother and at the age of forty-four had the mental faculties of a young girl. She was one of the sweetest, nicest human beings I've ever encountered, and whenever I'd see her walking around the neighborhood she'd smile and wave, and sometimes she'd even come over and play cars with me in the front yard.

That night I watched people walking our neighborhood, down the street and in our backyard. They walked up and down, up and down, and when it got dark they got flashlights and kept going, their lights flashing over every tree and bush and chain-link fence.

I didn't read my comic books and I didn't play my game. When it was time I got under the covers of my old brass bed but I didn't sleep. Mom wouldn't say what we were both thinking when she said good night. She didn't have to. I already knew something very bad had happened.

———

That summer Pam Foddrill's disappearance gripped the town of Linton. You couldn't go anywhere without worried conversations, breathless speculation, an inescapable sense of dread. There were rumors of a serial killer. Secondhand stories of a drifter who roamed the streets at night in search of a new victim. A psychic was brought in to try to divine where she might be and kept the local media rapt with every vision. My mother had a dream that Pam was next to a body of water and we drove to the forest one afternoon and searched for hours.

We worried over Pam for weeks. Outside her mother wept in front of their house and taped pictures of Pam on a gnarled tree that hung out over the road. All hours of the day she paced the cracked sidewalk. My mom watched her from our door, crying and shaking her head. At night, I prayed for Pam to return home safely before struggling to sleep, suffering one nightmare after another.

One evening as I lay in bed watching TV, something was odd. I felt watched, and the sensation instantly paralyzed me. I remember it was as if I moved even the slightest bit I might die. I tried to yell for my mom in the other room, but my voice couldn't rise above a whisper.

Then, a tapping at my window.

Tap.

Tap.

Tap.

The tapping sped up until it was a full-fledged knocking. I couldn't stay in bed anymore. I threw the covers off in a white-hot panic and ran into my mom's bedroom, where she was fast asleep after a long day's work. I shook her awake just in time for the sound to start on the window in her room.

Tap.

Tap.

Tap.

Almost every night for the next month and a half, a man stalked us with frightening regularity. He showed up nearly every day or else would call and whisper odd, sexual threats over the phone.

When the sun set, it was only a matter of when he'd show up and peep through our windows, knock on the glass, or, eventually, try to force his way in. We called the police several times, but they'd only come, walk the perimeter of our property, and then tell Mom she needed to stop calling them and invest in a gun.

The first time I caught a glimpse of him came one evening when we were sitting on the couch watching television. Mom had made a bowl of popcorn and put on some mindless show to pass the time. At one point, I went into the kitchen to get a drink, and on the way back through the dining room, I saw through the window a man hiding in the shadows.

As usual, Mom called the police while I grabbed a baseball bat. They came, asked a few questions, and then promptly left. It wasn't an hour before our phone was ringing. The neighbor from across the alley was calling to tell us the guy was back and peeping through the kitchen windows. Mom grabbed the bat and flew out the back door, sending the man running into the night.

He grew bolder. One night he tried to pry open the window in the bathroom around nine o'clock when we were obviously still up and milling around the house. Another time I snuck out of bed for a late-night snack, and as I was looking through the fridge, he knocked on the back door as if he were a regular visitor. I froze in fear, knowing I needed to get to my mom's room or find the bat to protect myself. Then he moved to the knob, trying to turn it or jostle the door loose. When that didn't work, he tried to batter his way in with his shoulder. That was enough to get me moving, and I sprinted through the house screaming as loud as I could.

I don't know why he stopped. Maybe he got tired of the game, maybe he was arrested for something else, but eventually the harassment came to an end, leaving us to return to our lives with a sickening feeling that things could've gotten a lot worse had he ever managed to get in. Twenty years later, Mom still talks about the scenarios that played out in her head, all of the appalling possibilities that seemed inevitable over the course of those six weeks. With Pam's disappearance lingering over our lives, we didn't need to think too hard to imagine what we avoided.

Months later, on December 2, outside Lawrenceville, Illinois, two hunters happened upon Pam's body. For nearly three years her murder remained unsolved until a prisoner in the Lawrence County Jail in Bedford, Indiana, named Roger Long bragged to his fellow inmates that he'd played a role in the crime. Soon, the investigation uncovered that Long, with the help of two other men—John Redman and Jerry Russell—and a pair of women they'd intimidated into helping—Wanda Hubbell and Plynia "Pixie" Fowler—had conspired to kidnap Pam, torture and rape her, and then eventually murder her.

The grisly details played out in our local paper, casting an awful pall on the town. Apparently the men had attempted to take Pam twice before, but succeeded after they'd coerced Pixie Fowler into wearing her Wendy's uniform—the restaurant was just down the street and, along with the IGA, one of the only places Pam was allowed to walk to on her own—and lured Pam close to their van, where they subdued her with a stun gun and drove away. They took her to Jerry Russell's dilapidated home just a block and a half away and confined her to a hot attic where they beat and raped her repeatedly for days, often using methamphetamines so they could keep at it for hours at a time. Eventually, they tired of her, killed her, and kept her in a shed for a few days before driving her body over the state line.

It was a senseless and brutal crime. Pam's elderly mother buckled under the weight of the tragedy and on the tree where she'd pasted pictures of Pam she began hanging macabre displays of the season's holidays, including beheaded Easter bunnies and hacked-apart Santa Clauses. She still paced the neighborhood, weeping openly and calling for her daughter. People in town shook their heads at the very mention of the crime, puzzling over just how they'd lived in close proximity to such monsters.

How, they asked, could anybody do such a thing?

————

Eight years later, they asked the same question when nineteen-year-old Katelyn Wolfe was murdered by Jordan Buskirk and Randal Crosley, twenty-five and twenty-six, respectively. The two young men said later they wanted to see what it was like to rape and murder a woman, it didn't matter who, and they'd driven forty miles to Terre Haute to a Gander Mountain store and a novelty shop to buy condoms, handcuffs, restraints, rope, and a twenty-pound weight to prepare for their crime. After strangling Wolfe to death, they sank her body in the state forest and then logged onto her phone and posted a Facebook status to try to throw police off their trail.

This crime, like Pam Foddrill's murder, was shocking in its senselessness. Commenters online speculated they'd been under the spell of Satan when they'd acted, something the churches in Linton had maintained following Pam's murder.

Then, a month later, news broke in California that twenty-two-year-old Elliot Rodger had murdered six people and wounded fourteen others, then killed himself. Before committing suicide, Rodger had sent a 107,000-word manifesto titled "My Twisted World: The Story of Elliot Rodger" to dozens of people and uploaded a video to YouTube called "Elliot Rodger's Retribution."

The documents, and all the crimes described here, are testaments to the dangers of toxic masculinity. In the manifesto Rodger writes extensively about being rejected by women, his peers calling him "names like 'faggot' and 'pussy,' typical things those types of scumbags would say," and the resulting humiliation. Because his fragile masculinity had been challenged, he resolved to punish the world.

His final missive, the unsettling video "Elliot Rodger's Retribution," takes place in the front seat of his black BMW, a swath of orange sunlight cutting across his young face as palm trees sway in the background. "Hi, Elliot Rodger here," he begins. "Well, this is my last video, it all has come to this. Tomorrow is the day of retribution, the day in which I will have my revenge against humanity."

As he mugs for the camera and laughs like a cut-rate supervillain, Rodger details the motivation for his planned rampage, summing it all up by putting the blame on women who have rejected his advances. "It's not fair," he says, "you girls have never been attracted to me. I don't know why . . . but I will punish you all for it. It's an injustice, a crime."

The plan was to enter "the hottest sorority house of UCSB [University of California Santa Barbara]" and "slaughter every single spoiled, stuck-up, blond slut I see inside there," which would show them that Rodger was ". . . the superior one, the true alpha male." He promises, "If I can't have you girls, I will destroy you."

At the heart of all this is a sense of entitlement that, once challenged, motivated Elliot Rodger to kill. Dr. Michael Kimmel, a sociologist whose research focuses on masculinity, calls this "aggrieved entitlement" and describes it in *Angry White Men* as "a sense that benefits to which you believed yourself entitled have been snatched away from you by unseen forces larger and more powerful."

When considering the ever-tenuous relationship between men and their masculinity, it's important to remember that any failure to live up to the unrealistic expectations of the gender are seen as personal failings, and thus the man suffering the crisis of identity must make a decision: Are the failings his fault or the rest of the world's?

With Elliot Rodger, the decision was obvious since he admitted as much in his own words. He couldn't understand why women had never found him attractive, or why the men in his life wouldn't accept him, so he decided to take out his anger and frustration on society because the problem had to be external. His focus on the Alpha Phi sorority house, where he was denied entry, then decided to shoot pedestrians outside, was about exerting his masculine privilege on women and their bodies. Considering the influence of masculinity, it is common for men like Rodger to think that women, the "weaker sex," are nothing more than objects men are entitled to. This means they should always give men their bodies, their sex, and, in too many cases, their lives.

These three crimes, though separated by decades and thousands of miles, are a result of that mindset. Pam Foddrill and Katelyn Wolfe in Linton, Indiana, and the women of Isla Vista were merely objects to be obtained and dominated. For the men perpetrating the crime, the kidnapping, torture, and rape of Foddrill had nothing to do with the woman enduring the abuse, and neither did the senseless killing of Wolfe. The women Rodger spoke of were unidentified, not a single individual named. They were transposable because, to men like these, it's not about the women they're hurting, it's about their own power and identity.

Rodger's declaration that "if I can't have you girls, I'll destroy you" sounds too much like the familiar "if I can't have you, nobody will" that has become synonymous with domestic abuse and intimate violence. When men are asserting control of women, the act is about property. It's the external as a symbol of the internal self-worth. Just as men lust after power, wealth, and material things as a means to symbolize their own worthiness, they're looking to control women for the same purposes.

Undoubtedly, unchecked toxic masculinity is one of the biggest threats to American women. Statistics have shown that one out of every five will be sexually assaulted; women make up 91 percent of all rape victims; and upward of 1,600 American women were murdered by men in 2015 alone.*† Some argue that testosterone is to blame and that men are biologically more violent, but science has proven this isn't the case. In fact, Dr. Frank McAndrew of Knox College argues there's only a "weak connection" between testosterone and violent behavior.‡

The nature argument of male violence would leave some to believe that this epidemic is untreatable, a side effect of sex differences, but the truth is much more complicated. In their childhood socialization men are taught that masculine characteristics are more desirable and feminine ones are unacceptable, thus rendering women as second-class citizens. Men with flagging masculinity, whether it's a result of personal failings in social status or, in Elliot Rodger's case, rejection of entitlement, lash out in violent ways because their only acceptable form of communication is to exhibit anger and violence.

These unthinkable crimes—rape, stalking, torture, murder—

---

* "Statistics of Sexual Violence," National Sexual Violence Resource Center, 2015, www.nsvrc.org/sites/default/files/publications_nsvrc_factsheet_media -packet_statistics-about-sexual-violence_0.pdf.

† Kali Halloway, "In Just One Year, More Than 1,600 Women Were Murdered by Men in the U.S.," *Ms. Magazine*, September 25, 2017, www.msmagazine .com/blog/2017/09/25/just-one-year-1600-women-murdered-men-u-s.

‡ Christopher Mims, "Strange but True: Testosterone Alone Does Not Cause Violence," *Scientific American*, July 2007, www.scientificamerican.com/article /strange-but-true-testosterone-alone-doesnt-cause-violence.

are extensions of a patriarchy in which men believe they are entitled to women in totality. They are stronger, better, and as "alpha males," they deserve everything they desire. In this system, women are seen as less than human, and this belief determines everything from our social and political lives to whether a woman is murdered or raped.

Simply put, the patriarchal system that devalues women can result in any number of trespasses, everything from economic discrimination to harassment, stalking to murder. The system is untenable, unachievable, and when people are forced to conform, the consequences can be deadly.

8

By the time I reached high school I was more confused than ever about how I fit into the masculine world. High school can be pure hell for anyone, let alone those still trying to find themselves. Being an outsider is almost unbearable. In my small school the hierarchy was visible with every stroll through the fluorescent-lit hallways. There were those who had come through puberty having accepted their place in the masculine structure, and then there were the rest of us who suffered.

There were four distinct personas a guy could embrace, all of which embodied acceptable stereotypes of manhood. There were the jocks who, more often than not, played football and behaved in predictably profane and jocular ways. Their antithesis was the prep, or a guy who came from a financially successful family, wore expensive clothes, and carried himself as the aristocracy of the school. Hicks were hardly ever seen without their Carhartts or John Deere hats with a fishhook on the bill. When they weren't in farming classes they were probably dipping Skoal by their rusted-out pick-ups blasting country music. And then there were the outlaws, who loved to fight, smoke, experiment with drugs, and generally search for reasons to instigate violence against anyone who might think they were better than them.

Of course, these personas were not always mutually exclusive. Plenty of hicks lettered as linemen, outlaws planted soybeans, and some jocks spent as much time suspended as they did in the huddle. Everyone who didn't fit snugly into one of those categories, or straddle the line, spent most of their time trying them on for size—a phenomenon, I should mention, that often continues into adulthood.

What I had learned about being a man from my grandpa had gotten me there, but no parts of my personality fit well into these available personas. I played sports, but couldn't stand the dumb-fuckery of my teammates. I was extremely poor, which ruled out being a prep, and shit out of luck when it came to being a hick, as my impoverished family lived on a run-down street populated with dilapidated houses and drug dens, not a family farm slipping into foreclosure. The outlaw life didn't appeal to me, as watching Jon sit in prison, and seeing the results of the callous men who killed my neighbor and tormented my mom, cured me of any desire to test the law.

What I wanted was to get out, go to college, and pursue my dream of being a writer. I bullshitted with my friends in the hallways and pretended not to care about anything, but in my classes I wasn't paying attention not because of apathy, but because I was too busy writing my own stories. At home, from the time I woke up to the time I went to sleep, I was either reading or watching old movies. I scribbled in notebooks and on receipts at my job as a cashier at Walmart.

To my father and the other men in my life it was a weak vocation, something a woman or a gay man might do, an embarrassing pastime I needed to grow out of. There was no room at home or in school for men to be creative or intelligent. Any attempt at either resulted in bullying, excommunication, or constant derision for being a "fag."

Eventually, I gave in and quit telling people I wanted to be a writer. My sophomore year, I signed up for football to try to find my place as a jock. In my town that sport is the second biggest religion after Baptist. What convinced me to play was that my first girlfriend told me that any guy who didn't suit up was a pussy, a sentiment my father had touted for years whenever the Colts were on TV.

Trying to score points with both of them, I joined the team and did my best to fit in, which wasn't easy, as football's culture, as anyone who's ever played can tell you, is a hotbed of hypermasculinity. In the locker room stereos blast AC/DC and Guns N' Roses—any song about murder or sex will do—while players strut around in various states of undress. As they compare their most recent sexual conquests, going into graphic detail about their exploits and the girls they've bedded, their demeanor changes. Gone is any filter they carry out in the open world. Their language turns gruff. They gloat about their sex, say racist and homophobic things, and challenge each other like rams in the wild. When Donald Trump defended his *Access Hollywood* banter as "locker room talk," this is exactly what he was referencing, and he wasn't wrong.

The sights and sounds of the locker room stay with you forever. Naked young men wrestling on the floor, in the shower, shoving each other into lockers, bullying underclassmen and any teammates labeled "soft" or a "fag" by beating them or emasculating them, whether it was with taunts or humiliating assaults, including holding them down and covering their faces with genitals or forcibly undressing them, ridiculing them, and threatening to violate them anally.

After we'd suited up, we'd clack outside in our cleats and pads to the field, where our coaches were waiting with a regimen of drills that would, in their words, "separate the men from the boys."

These drills, including bear crawls, sleds, drop-downs, and other strenuous activities, would have been bad enough in a vacuum, but as we worked out multiple coaches would be in our faces, berating us. It was nothing for a line coach to call us a bunch of girls, or single out a player and ask if they were on their period or if they were just tired from fucking their boyfriends all night.

Before the season we'd endure two-a-days, or two separate practices, often in hundred-degree heat and summer's stifling humidity. If we were overwhelmed we'd be singled out in front of our teammates. Breaking to get a drink of water was an embarrassment that could lead to being ostracized. If a player threw up or passed out? Weakness.

To that end, injuries were seen as a sign of fragility. To be a man, after all, was to be invincible. If you got hurt, it was a sign you weren't tough enough, meant you could lose your spot. Coach's first reaction to someone collapsing in a heap or falling lame was to tell them to rub some dirt on it, quit acting like a girl, or to walk it off, which was what I got told when I blacked out from a collision and later when my leg planted wrong and my kneecap dislocated.

It's this culture of hypermasculinity that has created an atmosphere that could lead to tragedies like the death of Jordan McNair, a lineman for the University of Maryland who died in 2018 from heatstroke.* Following that unnecessary death, details have emerged

---

* Darran Simon, "Jordan McNair, University of Maryland Football Player Who Died After Workout Didn't Receive Proper Care, Review Says," CNN, August 14, 2018, www.cnn.com/2018/08/14/us/university-maryland-football -player-death-review/index.html.

from Maryland that show a toxic culture permeated the program. To "motivate" their players, Maryland coaches routinely mocked them, questioned their masculinity, called them "pussy bitches," humiliated them in front of their teammates, and put them in unreasonable and unhealthy situations as punishment.*

When looking at the disgusting and dangerous world of football, many will ask why any young man would ever put up with the abuse. But what I can tell you, even years removed, is that the thing I'll remember until I die is how the game *could* make me feel. After a lifetime of being on the outside looking in, it was a miraculous joy to be accepted. When my teammates celebrated me, when my coaches gave me praise between the insults, when the town cheered, it made me feel as invincible as I was told I should be. Running over an offensive lineman, tackling a running back, and dominating another player was incredibly satisfying. Walking around town, and into school, in my red, white, and blue jersey reassured every single doubt I'd ever had about my masculinity, and, like any other drug, I wanted more.

With my knee in tatters, however, I'd have to find another way to get my fix.

———

Not long after I was injured, my house got connected to the internet. We'd hesitated at first because money was tight with Jon gone, but once he came home and married Mom, we connected to

---

* Heather Dinich, Adam Rittenberg, and Tom VanHaaren, "The Inside Story of a Toxic Culture at Maryland Football," ESPN, August 10, 2018, www.espn.com/college-football/story/_/id/24342005/maryland-terrapins -football-culture-toxic-coach-dj-durkin.

a modem and started browsing. In those days dial-up was remarkably slow, and our subscription limited us to an hour and a half of connection a day, which was mostly spent waiting for pages to load.

Having grown up without the internet, I didn't initially understand its appeal. There was email, which no one really used, and then badly constructed pages that hurt the eyes and were a chore to read. I knew the internet was a world-shattering invention only because the news told me that was the case, but as I sat there, watching my screen fill pixel by pixel in my mom's dining room, I still didn't quite get it.

Eventually, as the web filled out, its promise revealed itself. A friend of mine in biology gave me a URL written out on a torn sheet of notebook paper, and when I got home I logged on and waited dutifully while the address came to life. The page was aesthetically unappealing with dark blue links set against a black background, but the content, when I read it, was amazing. A handful of people my age were writing about movies, going in depth about their plots, symbolism, and misfires. It sounds trite to talk about it now, but back then, in 1997, this was a game-changer.

Before that the only things to read were books, newspapers, magazines, and comics, and the authors of those works felt totally removed from my everyday life. This page, this ugly site, represented a sea change. Suddenly I could read immediate reactions, find other people who enjoyed my hobbies, and—this was huge— interact with people my age who wrote and lived similar lives.

Almost overnight, the world expanded from my lonely little street in Linton, Indiana, to the rest of the world.

There were sites that served every hobby I had that I couldn't discuss with anyone else. There were pages about writing, about video games, about professional wrestling, and pages by, for, and about other young men who felt alone in their struggles.

Their front pages were all remarkably similar. A static background, links to articles written by personalities on the site, and then links to the forum where readers and writers could discuss their pieces or whatever caught their fancy. They were forebears of the blogs and sites we enjoy now, and served as places of respite for people like myself.

What was so welcoming was the fact that the internet was fueled by the written word. While my classmates talked about hating the new online world, I thrived in it. When I logged on, I could express myself better than nearly anyone else. I could write circles around the people who treated me badly and this opened a new opportunity that wouldn't come to fruition until much later. It would eventually change everything, challenging the last bastions of masculinity as creativity and expression, both necessary in the online world, suddenly trumped the physical prowess and emotional stoicism held most sacrosanct in the real one.

I earned opportunities to write on the main pages for several of the sites I'd been a fan of, garnering a decent following over the next few years. I made a number of friends in that time who had struggled with the expectations of patriarchal masculinity and found that a great majority of the people who frequented these sites were other sensitive, intellectual males who'd suffered as they fell short of what their fathers and peers wanted from them.

Over time, the sites gave way primarily to forums and the transition made sense. The original system was constructed to bring in like-minded individuals under the guise of hobbies and then create a microcosm where we could seek shelter and comfort. Eventually, the other hobby sites began falling by the wayside and conglomerating into larger forums that grew in size and gravity. These were sites like Something Awful and 4chan, places where tech-savvy creative types could amass and interact. At times the content was edgy or provocative, but it seemed like that edginess and provocation was all in good fun, a testing of limits that would never have consequences in the real world.

Though the sites seemed to be intended as an alternate reality where intellectuals could find new ways to thrive, soon the disease of toxic masculinity rendered that experiment null and void. There'd been elements present from the beginning. The sites encouraged competition over hits and readers, so alpha male confrontations and feuds weren't uncommon, though these fights were obviously settled with insults as opposed to violence. Our anonymity with our screen names and handles added to an atmosphere where posters could adopt a persona of their own invention. Many of them, as the guys in my school had done, were hypermasculine to the point of satire, many of them wildly offensive, distasteful, and cruel.

———

In June 2016 I went to a Donald Trump rally in Greensboro, North Carolina. At the time I'd been a fairly anonymous writer covering the campaign for something to do in his spare time. When I walked into the Greensboro Coliseum, nobody cared what I thought about politics.

What I witnessed that night was one of the most blatant displays of offensive, fascistic behavior I'd seen since my days in the locker room. It was like all of the troubling, frightening things that'd been saved for private spaces, kept behind locked doors, had suddenly exploded into the public arena. Society had kept these people at bay for years, or at least mostly contained by the threat of consequence, but Trump's candidacy had sprung the lock and given them safety in the daylight.

My reporting was among the first to sound the alarm as to just what had begun taking shape. Up until that point the criticism of Trump was that he was offensive, sure, unacceptable, certainly, but no one in their right mind thought he'd actually get elected. That rally, and the ones that followed, proved these thoughts to be depressingly misguided, and the certainty had only allowed his base of deplorables to take root.

In the days following my report, I began receiving attention, some positive, some worse than I could have imagined, as I, like the rest of the world, had yet to really lift up the rock that was the internet and get a good look at what was festering underneath.

Within days I'd had my life and livelihood threatened, and some of the most consistent and angriest voices were from a group of fringe white nationalists who, depending on their branch, toyed with the very fascism their grandfathers had fought against or embraced it wholeheartedly. There were different strains, including ethnonationalists, neo-Nazis, and members of the so-called Manosphere, a term meant to reflect areas of the web that had fixated on preserving the tenets of toxic masculinity. There were pick-up artists, red-pillers who believed the world was falling under a feminist-driven conspiracy, and blatant misogynists who reveled in publishing articles discussing how to properly train women for their own use.

Dedicated to Donald Trump, these men have attacked me for years now, especially whenever I grew curious as to who they were and began investigating and reporting on their corners of the internet. Almost to a person they resorted to the same type of bullying I'd seen when I was younger. They made fun of my appearance, questioned my sexuality, and attempted to emasculate me. The environment was incredibly juvenile, and the closer I looked the more I discovered why: the forums I'd been a part of in my high school days, stocked with insecure men desperate to overcompensate, had continued to degenerate into cesspools of unchecked toxic masculinity.

On those boards, other outcast males had gathered, and despite their having sought asylum from a masculine world that had rejected them, they'd gone on to create their own patriarchal reality that not only reinforced the old expectations, but supercharged them. In an effort to out-alpha-male the other posters, young men competed with one another as to who could say the most offensive things, display the least amount of emotion or concern, and share the ugliest memes and content they could find or create. They generally sought to portray themselves as hardened men.

These personas were a new means of finding themselves. No longer did they have to be jocks, preps, hicks, or outlaws, though the latter certainly was a precursor and foundation of this new man: the troll.

In the digital age, the troll is essentially a caricature and embodiment of all the worst traits associated with masculinity. They're culturally and intellectually shallow. Angry. Violent. Aggressive. And, after years of wading through graphic images, postmodern stew, racist propaganda, and disgusting and misogynistic pornography, they have grown into nihilists with no other purpose besides punishing the world while laughing to prove they're stronger than their humanity.

Just as other men struggle to tell the difference between reality and cultural illusion, trolls are incapable of determining where the internet ends and real life begins. Their exploits have emerged from the forums that incubated them and into society at large. They attack feminism and progressivism wherever they're found, threaten to murder and rape women, intimidate journalists, and have coalesced into a political base that eventually elected the president of the United States of America.

They make great shows of their overcompensation. They call opponents "cuck" after the old emasculating term "cuckold," rant and rave about "beta males" and "soy boys," and generally oppose any facet of culture that's supported by progressives, be it pop culture or academic thought. In retaliation, they undermine anything disagreeable and organize mass actions that culminate in harassment, like what was seen in the ludicrous "Gamergate" controversy when misogynist video game fans systematically harassed and threatened female journalists. They embrace their own collection of "intellectuals" who've created a more masculine-friendly worldview, undermine the existence of rape culture with bogus statistics, push ethnocentric worldviews with fake science, and pay their hard-earned money to "experts" like Mike Cernovich, a California man who preaches the gospel of "gorilla mindsets" and warns supporters not to be "beta males."

The patriarchy that hurt these men in the first place has been, and will continue to be, reinforced by their own hand. Sometimes, when I'm feeling lost or hopeless, I log onto the old websites where I'd once found comfort as a lost young man and the new ones that have taken their place and I see the conversations haven't changed. I recognize the men having them, the trolls populating those boards, and think about how easily I could've become one of them.

It is, after all, a constant struggle not to succumb to toxic masculinity for any man who's grown up surrounded by it. For many of us, it was the reality we were raised on, a reality that defines how we think, a reality where patriarchal power and privilege serve as a foundation for not just how we see the world but how we conduct ourselves, particularly when we are at our worst. Insecurity can open the door for any number of behaviors and can lead to terrible consequences, whether it's an existence spent drowning in toxic masculinity or the cold, gray walls of prison, and regardless of how much progress we've made, or how we've fought against the current, we're always just one wrong move away from succumbing once more.

II

MY FATHER'S SON

9

When the officer shined his flashlight in my face, I shut my eyes tight and took a steadying breath. A few moments before I'd nearly plowed my vehicle into a nearby pole when the patrol car's lights had flashed blue and red, one of the most frightening sights I could ever imagine. I was drunk, extremely drunk, and when he'd whipped out of a parking lot and got on my tail I'd had no doubt what was coming. The realization that I was going to be arrested swept over me, and I began shaking so hard my teeth clicked.

"Why don't you come on back into my car for a second?"

I did as he asked and stumbled back to his cruiser, expecting any moment for cuffs to bite into my wrists, to be hauled off to the Jackson County Jail. I was surprised when he gestured for me to climb into the passenger seat. When the door shut, he turned off the red and blue lights.

Adrenaline flooded in and tussled for control with the alcohol, resulting in a bizarre mixture of intoxication and hyperawareness. I was both out of it and extremely cognizant of my situation. A sea of buttons blinked on the car's dash, a buzzing voice squawked over the radio. I was sitting in an idling cop car after being nailed dead to rights for drinking and driving, yet we weren't heading for jail. I hadn't been asked to blow into a Breathalyzer or walk a straight line. The whole situation felt like a fever dream. Real, but disconnected from reality.

"What've you been up to tonight?"

The question was surprisingly casual, small talk that made no sense in our current context. I admitted to having a few drinks in the neighboring city of Carbondale. I said I'd been out with my colleagues in Southern Illinois University's MFA program, which was technically true and also inaccurate. Sure, they'd been there, drinking at their usual table in the back, but I hadn't joined them. As usual I sat at the bar, where I drank a pitcher of beer before turning to whiskey. I'd drunk quickly and heavily, fully aware I was in full view of my cohorts and hoping they'd notice. I was playing the masculine role as I'd been taught as a boy. Hard. Stoic. Brooding and self-damaging. As I nursed my last drink, an acquaintance had come up to say hello and ask if I was okay. Happy the display had done its job, and satisfied with myself, I settled my tab and ended up behind the wheel.

What I didn't tell the officer was that I'd driven the eight miles with my windows down, the radio cranked up, and my foot glued to the accelerator. I'd gotten used to motoring that stretch after a night of boozing and with the Rolling Stones' *Let It Bleed* blaring, Keith Richards's guitar screaming and Mick Jagger howling, I'd felt alive and vibrant. I felt dangerous. I felt cool.

I felt like a completely different person. Like a man.

As I struggled between blacking out and a panic attack in the cop car, I couldn't help but think of my father and all his drinking and driving stories. They were legends in my family, the bedrock of "Old John," a mythical figure who drank and ran himself ragged and survived years of drunken driving accidents. He'd wrecked every car he'd ever owned, launched a truck off a turn and landed in the waiting arms of a tree, had destroyed miles' worth of road signs driving back from a bar in Terre Haute in an incident that supposedly made the evening news. He'd done all of this and lived to tell the tale.

It occurred to me that my situation was one John Sexton might find himself in.

It was a thought I was starting to have more and more often. I was acting like my dad, taking risks like him. Hell, I was even starting to look like him.

"What's going on?"

I turned to the officer and tried to steady myself. "What's going on?"

"In your life," he said. "What's going on that made you go out and get wasted like this?"

Slurring and struggling to make my thoughts cohesive, I tried to explain. I told him about how I'd screwed up two relationships in the past year because I couldn't get my shit together. I told him about my struggles in graduate school, how I felt disrespected and alone. It only felt like whining because I was whining, and despite my pathetic complaints the officer nodded as he listened.

"If you ask me," he said, "it sounds like you've got a lot to lose."

"I guess you're right."

"There's no guessing about it. Pulling the shit you pulled tonight? That's a hell of a way to lose everything."

"I guess."

"No guessing."

To my surprise, after I'd sobered up a bit he asked where I lived and when I told him it wasn't more than a mile down the street he wanted to know if I thought I could drive that far if he followed. Then I was back in my car and on the road, the cruiser trailing closely behind. In the driveway of the depressing duplex I was subleasing, I stood slack-jawed as the officer motored past.

I've come to understand how fortunate I was that night. The officer who pulled me over had taken pity on me and granted me a chance that was predicated on mercy and unbelievable privilege, a privilege that has long been a courtesy between law enforcement and white men. But, a few minutes removed, I was still lost in the fog of self-pity. Inside I grabbed another beer out of the fridge and puzzled over what'd just happened. Instead of its being a miraculous moment or a crossroads where I could choose to better my life, it was just more proof of how awful things had gotten. I polished off the beer, grabbed the last of the six-pack, and staggered into the bedroom.

With all the hangings and decorations still belonging to the duplex's official renters, the place never felt like home. There were pictures of the happy couple in their early days, snapshots of them on vacation and sickeningly in love, family portraits with brothers and sisters, the long-married parents they'd made proud. Glancing at them, it seemed like everyone else had their lives in order but me.

I cried for a bit while I nursed that last beer. I hated myself for being so weak, for crying. I thought of what a soft little boy I'd been, the boy all the men around me hated and beat and criticized. I'd been an outsider, an outcast, but somehow the socialization and conditioning I'd endured still held sway over me. At that point, at that late of an hour, it seemed obvious what I needed to do. Climbing off the bed, I got on the floor and searched for the .22-caliber rifle I kept hidden under there. When I found it, I laid it and its clip of bullets on the comforter.

My dad had given me that gun, my first one, the year before. Like he'd taught me, I locked the clips into the rifle and cocked the bolt. For a long time I held it in my hands, my fingers tracing the trigger as I imagined what the world might look like without me. My mother would be heartbroken, but in that state all I could think about were the people who'd probably be relieved not to have to deal with my bullshit anymore. How much of a reprieve it would be not to hurt the way I did.

Luckily, I blacked out. I'd sat there stewing for god knows how long over how bad things had gotten, what a miserable state I was in, until I fell asleep with the gun cradled in my lap. Imagining what it would be like to pull the trigger, the question the cop had asked made laps in my head. A question I couldn't even begin to answer.

What's going on?

What's going on?

———

My father remained a distant figure throughout my childhood. I'd see him occasionally around town, visit his house every now and then, but whenever we were together he seemed uneasy. At his home he was always in another room or outside, and the few words that passed between us were strained and uncomfortable. He was obviously ashamed of me, so much so that sometimes when I happened to meet his friends they were shocked to find out he had a son at all.

I had every reason to want nothing to do with him. I knew all the stories about him and my mom, how badly he had treated her, and his absence and lack of interest in me never ceased to be an insult; but like many kids of divorce, the pain of being abandoned lingered and hurt me in ways I couldn't begin to understand. I couldn't help but wonder what was so wrong with me that my own father didn't want to have a relationship. There must have been something defective, something that wasn't quite right that kept him away. I tried to prove myself time and again, whether it was in the classroom or playing sports, but nothing seemed to make a difference. I kept coming back to his disappointment that I wasn't tough. Soon it was clear that my status as an interloper in the masculine world was most certainly playing a large part in our strained relations.

But then, when I was seventeen, we had what could only be considered a breakthrough.

I was standing in a rental store in Linton, trying not to puke, when my dad surprised me. Normally I would've noticed him come in the door, but I was the most hungover I'd ever been. The night before I'd partied with a group of people I barely knew, getting hammered to the point of oblivion. To my surprise we ended up in an abandoned house where we sat on the floor and lay waste to several cases of Bud Light and a few bottles of Goldschläger. I didn't want to admit it, but I'd been frightened that we'd get caught breaking and entering. Not frightened enough to walk away, though. I knew this was what I was supposed to do. Men were supposed to go out drinking. They were supposed to get shit-faced and take risks.

"Long night?" my dad asked, scaring me out of a stupor.

Normally Dad avoided me. I'd seen him do it multiple times. At Walmart or at a game, he'd make himself scarce to avoid having to talk. But that afternoon he seemed eager.

"I guess," I answered, still unsure what was happening.

"Yeah?" he said. "You drink a little too much?"

My first thought was that I was in trouble. The idea was ludicrous, though. My dad had nothing to do with me, much less any sway over whether I got punished for anything. "Maybe," I said.

"Huh." He worked his tongue in his cheek and smiled. "Where'd you hang out last night? Some house out in the country?"

I went cold. Somehow Dad had caught me and I didn't have even the beginning of an idea how. After some questioning he finally let me in on the joke. His buddies at the police department had gotten a tip the night before about our party and were about to bust us when one of them called Dad and told him his son was in the house. Doing him a favor, the police left us alone. Looking back now, it's incredible how many times I could have had my life derailed if it weren't for the distinct contrast in how law enforcement treats white men and everyone else.

But Dad wasn't interested in what laws I'd broken or how close I'd come to real and serious trouble. He wanted to hear about the party, so we stood in the store for a good half hour as he asked for the blow-by-blow. What'd I drink? Did I talk to any girls? Were we getting high? With every confirmation he loosened up more and more. At one point he shook his head and said, "I didn't think you had it in ya!"

Eventually we went outside and lingered by his truck. Dad had moved on to telling his stories about his exploits, the same ones I'd been hearing for years. Only now, they were more detailed. He was filling in the blanks that'd always been there, revealing the specifics about those years he'd been out running while Mom and I struggled. All the drinking and all the women. There was a brief tinge of resentment as I listened, but I was mostly just relieved my dad was talking to me.

"Welp," he said, checking his watch, "reckon I ought to get out of here. Thought I'd come in and chew on your ear a bit. Get the inside scoop on what you kids were up to last night."

I couldn't help but beam. Dad had come into the store just to talk to me. He'd seen my car and deliberately sought me out. This was night and day from our usual dynamic, as different as different could be.

Rolling down the window in his truck, he leaned on the door. "Swing by one of these days. I'll tell you some more stories."

"Sure," I said. "Sounds good."

Dad turned the key and his truck roared to life. Out of the speakers came the sound of Johnny Cash lamenting Sunday morning coming down. Dad asked if I liked Cash, or any of his outlaw pals, and I told him I did even though I'd heard only a few of the songs on the radio. After Dad had motored down the road I went straight to Walmart and spent what little money I had on a greatest hits record. I turned it up in my car, noticed a disapproving glance from the person in the parking spot next to me, and felt, for the first time in years, like I'd finally done something right.

———

That afternoon planted the seed of a crisis. Even just a fleeting moment of approval from my father was enough to set me in a direction that would irrevocably change my life. I'd been searching for years for shortcuts to acceptance. Fitting in as a man was an impossible task, a Sisyphean effort that could never be conquered. As a boy the masculine world seemed alien and incomprehensible with its jumble of contradictory expectations. Every one of the men around me had seemed in conflict with themselves and the world. In high school, none of the available personas offered any comfort. I'd resolved, by the time I turned eighteen, to live outside of the paradigm, had decided masculinity, with all its warts and foibles, was something I could simply opt out of.

What I didn't know then, and what I'm only coming to understand nearly twenty years later, is that because patriarchal masculinity is built into the structure of society, there is no such thing as opting out. It lies dormant in every man, regardless of his acceptance or denial. It permeates everything, reverberating throughout our language and tainting our power structure; it plagues our every action and thought. Because it is presented as reality from our nascent beginnings, it continually colors our perception regardless of how we might fight against its influence.

Toxic masculinity is a chronic illness, and once we're infected we always carry it with us.

My path from a sensitive misfit boy to the drunken man in a cop car was a road paved with innate conditioning, preconceived notions, blatant rationalizations, a desire to be accepted, painful insecurity, and the persistent delusion that I had somehow overcome my upbringing and escaped the gravity of my patriarchal role models. But I was woefully mistaken. The trauma I'd survived, the conditioning I'd been subject to, the soiled reality I'd been living and breathing throughout my upbringing, would continually plague me, perhaps even for the rest of my life.

———

As the first in my family to attend a university, I was convinced that I'd avoided these pitfalls. I'd always expected that first moment of college to feel like a victory of sorts. I'd fantasized about it my entire life, had imagined the day with so much excitement, but immediately I knew that everything wasn't fine because, within seconds of parking my car, I was overcome with a panic that made it hard to breathe or walk.

That anxiety followed me to my first class, then my second and third, and it didn't subside until I'd left the college in my rearview mirror. It continued every single time until I began skipping my courses and avoiding campus altogether. My grades that first semester were terrible because I wasn't able to focus on my studies or anything besides my irrational fears. I sank into a deep depression and was convinced that I'd squandered my one chance to make something of myself and escape the family and town that'd plagued me for years. I thought, with that escape, I'd be able to find myself and a new, better kind of way, and I hadn't found anything of the sort.

In the summer that followed my freshman year, I made myself a promise. I'd double down on my education, face my fear head-on, see if I could cut it as a student. If I failed, if I couldn't make it, I'd kill myself. It was that simple, and the logic of it seemed indisputable. Since I'd learned about suicide as a little kid, it had always seemed like an option. The story I'd told myself about my life—that I'd go off to college and leave my painful upbringing behind, finally make something of myself, and find a place where I could be happy and comfortable—seemed much more complicated now, like it might not come true, and if that were the case then what was the sense of living?

To tackle that year, I tried something different. I took what little money I'd saved from my jobs and bought some flannels and a pair of boots. I grew a beard. I actively worked to turn myself into a version of the men I'd grown up fearing. And when I arrived on campus I told myself I was someone different than the frightful young man who'd failed so miserably. This guy was tougher. He didn't worry what anyone thought of him and he certainly wasn't soft. Maybe I didn't realize it at the time, but I was trying to grow into the man they wanted me to be.

This sounds preposterous to an extent. The idea of transforming based on how you dress and carry yourself feels superficial, but it made an incredible difference. Though I knew deep down I was still the same boy who'd never fit in, the soft kid who'd disappointed most every man he ever knew, I was able to lose myself in the role and fake it enough to make it through the day. I strolled into class and pretended I didn't care about anything. I practiced the nonchalant air the men around me projected, I stifled my natural inclination to talk and express myself.

In turn, this is how I met my first group of college friends. Because they hadn't known me my entire life, I could be whoever I wanted with them. They didn't need to know my secret shame. They could think I was tough, a little dangerous. With them, I was the guy who might make a show out of drinking Jack Daniel's straight from the bottle. At the bars, I was the guy who got liquored up and didn't shy away from a confrontation. I got aggressive. And even though I was performing, and even though I knew deep down the whole thing was a charade, I couldn't help but take pride in the changes nonetheless.

Sometimes, out and about, loaded or else high from copious amounts of pot, I'd think of my dad, my stepdads, my high school peers. All of them had seen me for what I was. A sensitive, soft kid. A mama's boy afraid of his own shadow. If they could only see me now, I'd think, and with each new exploit, each new instance of gambling with my health, slowly the line between who I was pretending to be and who I really was began to disappear.

I started thinking like somebody else. The performance turned to mimicry and that mimicry became deeply rooted. I had constructed a shell, a hardened exterior meant to hide my vulnerabilities, and after wearing it enough I molded to the casing. This, I've come to learn, is how toxic masculinity works. Most every man suffers for his inability to live up to the rigors of masculinity as a child, and most every man feels like an outsider. But they build up that shell at a much earlier age, and they conform to it as the years pass. The performance continues until there's no performance anymore. There's just a man who knows no other way.

I knew better, though. After being raised by my mother and having seen my grandpa buck the trend, I was well aware there were alternatives. Later, when I followed my childhood dream of becoming a writer, I was taught to explore my empathy and creativity, two abilities that are often gendered and ruled as unmanly. I took classes in feminist literature and feminist thought, I joined a feminist group on campus because I had seen the way my mother had been treated by men her entire life. Even as I performed the masculine role, I knew the dangers of it and of a world predicated on dangerous masculine impulses.

The struggle to maintain the persona that made my attendance at college possible while also continuing my education was a difficult one. I had moments of deep shame for pretending to be something I wasn't, particularly as the realities of the patriarchy were made clearer with every book I read.

I was able to live in denial of my duplicity because I remained skeptical even as I wore the persona like armor. With horror I could see how masculinity plagued our country, especially in the spring of 2003 as I watched the Bush administration push its war against Iraq. I was convinced the invasion wasn't only illegal but also somehow influenced by the same rampant insecurity and predilection for violence I'd seen growing up.

This suspicion began as, in the wake of September 11, I'd witnessed my friends consumed by a fever for war. Even as the Twin Towers fell they were lusting for retribution, several of them hoping we'd see a nuclear bomb dropped or another country wiped off the map before the end of the day. They were obviously overcompensating for their fear, their anxiety, and their reliance on aggression was akin to how all the men I'd known had behaved whenever they felt vulnerable or weak.

In the days and weeks that followed there was a marked change in their behavior. Their conversations were more aggressive. They played violent video games while shouting racist slurs against Arabs; they fought each other and got into altercations nearly everywhere we'd go. There was a direct correlation between the tragedy of 9/11 and the escalation of their hypermasculine performativity.

Back home the effect was amplified as my male relatives reacted to the attacks by removing any and all filters and embracing their worst instincts. The racism was never-ending. They didn't even bother to hide it anymore. They freely espoused fascist ideals, talked about rounding up Muslim Americans and murdering them in cold blood, dreamed about genocide. Men just like them would go on to commit hundreds of hate crimes against Muslim Americans, a revolting trend that would reappear following the election of Donald Trump.*

Again, I was able to live in denial of my own issues because I still knew this was wildly problematic. I'd gotten accustomed to the surface-level performativity while retaining the good sense to understand how wrong this reaction was. This meant I was able to deny the work I needed to do personally while actively working to combat this new crisis of masculinity.

The lead-up to the Iraq War was predicated on harnessing this insecurity and the perceived need for retribution, a fact that has been proven in subsequent studies that showed threatened men sup-

---

* Kuang Keng Kuak Ser, "Data: Hate Crimes Against Muslims Increased After 9/11," PRI.org, September 12, 2016, www.pri.org/stories/2016-09-12/data -hate-crimes-against-muslims-increased-after-911.

ported the conflict more than others.* You could tell it was baked into the strategy as the Bush administration attempted to conflate al-Qaeda and Saddam Hussein, a racist and xenophobic appeal with no basis in reality. Even though I was an active participant in the antiwar movement, a self-styled revolutionary, I remained oblivious to my own shortcomings.

Again, my father served as a barometer in regard to how well I had acclimated to being a man. At that time, Dad was as fervently pro-war as anyone I knew. He talked constantly about the need to level the Middle East, a plan that would have meant the death of millions of innocent men, women, and children, and whenever I'd try to reason with him he'd quickly get angry and let me know how disappointed he was.

There was a particular incident in the time before the invasion that still sticks with me. I was visiting home from college for the weekend and had stopped by for a rare visit. Some relatives were there for dinner, and like always, the men soon changed the conversation to talk of war. One of my male relatives got on the subject of constitutional rights and how Muslims and antiwar activists should all be summarily stripped of their liberties. I spoke up and before I could get a full sentence out a pileup ensued. I was being called all those old familiar names—"pussy," "faggot," "queer"—as well as one that had only been inferred in the past.

"You're a traitor. That's what you are. A traitor."

The man who said it slammed his fist down on the table for emphasis. I looked around for support and found none. My own father, in his silence, seemed to agree.

---

* Dan Aloi, "Men Overcompensate When Their Masculinity Is Threatened, Cornell Study Shows," *Cornell Chronicle*, August 2005, news.cornell.edu/stories /2005/08/men-overcompensate-when-masculinity-threatened.

Before I left that afternoon, I walked out to my dad's garage, where he was tinkering with a car and sipping a beer. His demeanor had markedly changed. Our thawing of tensions had ended.

I told him I was taking off and what I got in response was a shaking of his head. He was leaning against a wall, a poster behind him of a bald eagle sharpening its talons as it watched the World Trade Center burn on television. Using President George W. Bush's now-infamous words, my own father said to me, "If you're not with us, you're against us." I tried to fight back against that ludicrous logic, but Dad cut me off by spitting on the concrete floor and saying, disgustedly, "You really are your mother's son."

I got in my car and drove back to Terre Haute, hating myself for again failing to be a man, feeling every bit the traitor I'd been accused of being.

10

For months there was radio silence. I didn't return to Dad's house and when we'd happen upon each other he was back to avoiding me. Seemingly we'd finally returned to normal as our brief attempt at a relationship had run its course. I'd just given up on hearing from him again when he called on a Sunday and left an awkward voicemail.

"Hey," it began, "it's ... uh ... it's ... Dad. Give me a call when you get the chance. Got something I wanna run by you."

I had to listen a few times over. The message was odd, and not just because my father was so obviously uncomfortable calling himself "Dad." He'd never left a voicemail before. And he'd sure as hell never wanted to run anything by me.

When he answered my call he was crunching some chips and seemed excited. "Hey!" he said, and paused to swallow. In the background I could hear the revving of engines from that afternoon's NASCAR race on his TV. "Need your opinion."

My dad had never asked my opinion on anything. Ever. His sentences were declarative or else directing his thoughts to whatever subject he wanted to talk about.

"Whatcha think about me running for mayor?"

"Of Linton?"

"You bet," he said before getting started on another handful of chips. "Reckon you and me could win this thing easier than shit."

What I pieced together over the next hour was that a major sea change had taken place back in my small hometown since I'd moved away for school. Jimmy K. Wright, a legendary Lintonian who'd served as mayor for twenty years and enjoyed a stature among young kids akin to George Washington, had just been unseated in the Democratic primary by a local businessman named Tom Jones. The upset was of historic proportions, but not completely unpredictable. Wright's health had been in decline and Jones's bona fides were above reproach. He owned the local sporting goods store, was a fixture in every major community organization, had retired as a coal miner, the job that defined Linton's personality, and had won the Greene County Open golf championship four times, a Babe Ruthian accomplishment if ever there was one.

"I don't know," Dad said when I told him I didn't think he could win. "Something tells me we've got a chance."

The word "we" kept popping up. Everything plural. Everything wrapped around the two of us. When I asked what he meant, Dad would say, "We've got this," or "We're gonna do this thing."

I knew Dad shouldn't become mayor. I tried to tell him as much without being hurtful. His politics were beyond problematic, and quite simply, he wasn't ready for the job. Most likely he would lose and lose badly.

But he had called me.

He'd asked me for my help.

"I need you in this," he said.

I need you.

The first time he'd ever expressed needing me, said anything even remotely like that. Of course I was going to say yes.

———

Our headquarters were housed in my dad's dental lab, a claustrophobic building roughly ten yards from his front porch. It was divided into three rooms, the workspace where he and his longtime partner Nancy polished and repaired false teeth, a bathroom, and a tiny office where I strategized and created campaign materials. It wasn't an ideal location for an upstart organization: dust from the work hung in the air and coated everything, the stink of chemicals so strong it watered the eyes, and the office itself was stuffed full of knickknacks my pack-rat dad collected. There were ticket stubs from IU games in the 1980s, off-brand Hot Wheels cars, dented Wheaties boxes, commemorative Pepsi cans bearing Jeff Gordon's likeness, half-deflated autographed basketballs, and chunks of notebook paper signed by drag racers in the ghostly Friday night lights at the Tri-State Speedway. Maneuvering was almost impossible, and nearly every movement resulted in an avalanche of junk.

Searching through a desk drawer overflowing with receipts and magazines, Dad said, "Here, first things first, let's get our logo picked out."

The catalogue he handed me was torn and wrinkled, the pages full of yard signs, t-shirts, and paraphernalia designed to help a candidate make a splash. I chose a red and white sign reading VOTE

SEXTON MAYOR and designed a matching shirt bearing the promise YOUR VOTE COUNTS.

"That's sharp," Dad said and then flipped the page. "Now, how about a few of these?"

His finger rested on a cheap-looking baseball hat I couldn't imagine anyone wanting, but he promised by the end of the month all his buddies he ate breakfast with every morning at McDonald's would be wearing one. He was right, and that's how we came to order a generic-looking red cap with white lettering that said SEXTON FOR MAYOR (a dead ringer for the MAKE AMERICA GREAT AGAIN hat that would show up over a decade later).

That was enough work for one day, he decided, and we got in his truck to deliver false teeth to dentists around Greene County. Dad's vehicles were as messy as his office. He had a penchant for dachshunds and so stuffed toys lined his dash. On the floor were mounds of wrappers from candy bars and empty cups from his multiple runs to McDonald's for iced tea. Alan Jackson sang over the radio about the tragedy of 9/11 and not knowing the difference between Iraq and Iran.

We'd gotten to the city limits when Dad reached into his pocket and dug out a tiny one-hitter with a golden pipe. He offered it to me and, surprised, I ground the pipe into some of the oldest and dirtiest weed I would ever smoke.

I was shocked. My dad's outlaw days, I'd thought anyway, belonged to the past. His years of raising hell, getting into bar fights, and drunk driving seemed like they'd taken place in another lifetime. The dad I knew drank a few beers here and there, but hung out with the city's police officers and talked at length about drug users and criminals getting their just due.

We passed the pot back and forth a few times, and with each turn I felt the old difficulties between us evaporating. When we were done with deliveries we came back to town and grabbed a table at a restaurant. Dad ordered us some beer and asked how school had been. I started telling him about my classes, but he laughed and said he wanted to hear about the drinking, the chasing of girls, the hell I was raising. As I offered up the details I could tell Dad was in a good mood and relieved to have a son who was turning into a real man. Soon he was getting into his own stories.

I'd heard most of them before. They were institutions in my family, legends that spanned decades and painted Dad as a flawed and troubled hero. He told me about barroom brawls in a Terre Haute dive called Simrell's that I went to every now and then, about his run-ins with women and the law, drunken fights he'd survived by luck alone. The stories didn't sound as pathetic and ridiculous as they had in the past. Bonding with my dad gave them a sheen, made them feel like a how-to guide to being a man. His bringing me in was the first time I'd ever felt accepted by him, and nothing he did, not even wearing a hat identifying as a Marine Corps veteran, a claim I knew was technically true but also misleading, mattered right then. That night we picked up a case of beer and drank and smoked like a couple of old buddies. I felt so relieved I almost forgot his mistreatment of my mother and that he'd had next to nothing to do with me for twenty-one years.

Already I could feel our new chumminess having an effect. Dad didn't seem like such a parody anymore; he felt like an attainable goal in terms of being a man. Already I was on the path to being tough and masculine; it wasn't so far-fetched anymore. Not so unachievable.

A few nights later, back in Terre Haute, I made a point of going to Simrell's, where I ordered my beer a pitcher at a time while shooting pool, just like my dad had done twenty years earlier.

My doubt about my persona had melted away and left me feeling tough again. Before hanging out with my dad it'd all felt so phony, so forced, but now it was just carrying on the family tradition. I mouthed off to everyone I came across, hoping someone would try me. One guy got pissed about my shit-talking over a game and got right in my face, close enough I could smell the beer on his breath. I was ready to lay into this stranger and beat him until my knuckles bled, and when the moment came he was the one who walked away.

As I came down from my adrenaline high, I thought of how proud my dad would be when I recounted the whole thing Monday morning.

————

Dad's candidacy for mayor was a losing battle. On election night we'd fall to Tom Jones to the tune of 1,505 votes to a paltry 454. The outcome, in retrospect, was inevitable, as the politics in my hometown were fairly predictable and my dad had no clue what he was doing. Though my father was good one-on-one and could bullshit with the best of them, he was a terrible campaigner who became so visibly nervous he put off potential voters and donors.

A few months in I think both of us could read the writing on the wall. Dad had stopped lining up campaign events and was quick with an excuse whenever invited to speak to groups or organizations. He sent me a few times in his place and, suffice it to say, as a twenty-one-year-old kid with a mop of hair and an overgrown beard, I made a woefully inadequate surrogate. Even as we approached the day of our political reckoning, we still met in his office to talk strategy for a few minutes before spending time together.

That was one of the gifts of that doomed campaign. In the midst of it all my dad started to like me for the first time. Because I wasn't as soft anymore, because I was willing to sit around and act like a traditional guy instead of trying to communicate or overthink things, he started trusting me more, and instead of simply dismissing my opinion he was seeking it. In doing so he realized I occasionally knew what I was talking about. And he was surprised, I think, to find that I wasn't the weak little kid he'd disliked for years. Suddenly we were just a couple of guys who could hang out.

We now spent most of our nights drinking and watching whatever game was on in his living room or else we'd head out to the country, get in some camping chairs, and fish out at the stripper pits and lakes. For hours we'd drink and smoke and shoot the shit with only crickets and cicadas to keep us company, Dad telling me about all his old exploits while I tried to keep pace with mine.

Our activities were always expressly gendered. When we were together it was with an air of performativity. Dad still talked a big game, continually referenced his questionable experiences as a Marine, still toed the conservative line, and when we had political conversations he was quick to condemn "pussy" ideas like climate change, welfare, civil liberties—basically anything that constituted caring for other people or worrying over consequences—positions researchers have now linked to performative masculinity.* I'd still challenge him, as I was coming from a considerably liberal perspective, but rather than insult me he now changed the subject to

---

* Aaron R. Brough and James E. B. Wilkie, "Men Resist Green Behavior as Unmanly," *Scientific American*, December 2017, www.scientificamerican.com /article/men-resist-green-behavior-as-unmanly.

something less confrontational, usually drinking or living in the fast lane.

That changed one day when I got back to the office after making a speech and he told me to change clothes and meet him outside. Before I knew it we were on the road and he was driving us deep into the country, down some old mine roads where the gravel kicked up and clattered against the sides of his truck. A mile or two back we came to a dead end where a handful of other trucks were parked and half a dozen men I recognized were standing around the tailgate of a Ford Ranger. When Dad got out they all greeted him with "There's the mayor!," a call that'd become the norm the moment he'd thrown his hat into the ring. We joined them and I assumed the posture I'd learned from years of observing men: arm draped over the edge of the truck's bed, body slumped like I'd just worked a full backbreaking shift, eyes casually surveying the scene like I didn't expect anything out of the ordinary but was still on watch.

As I looked around I saw something surprising. There, in the bed of the Ford, was a pile of guns. Pistols, shotguns, rifles, semi-automatics, guns fitted with scopes and silencers. A veritable arsenal that looked like it belonged to an army rather than a bunch of guys out target shooting.

Dad owned a lot of guns, so I wondered if we'd come all the way out to the country to maybe buy or trade, but then the men picked their weapons, loaded them, and carried them over to a makeshift range. Down the road, in front of a pile of dirt and gravel, they'd set up beer bottles, Mountain Dew cans, paint buckets, and human-shaped targets, including one with the likeness of Osama bin Laden.

Never before had I fired a gun. I'd held them, learned to clean them, even got taught how to sight, but until that day I'd never squeezed a trigger. The first one I shot was a .22 rifle. Just a simple thing with little to no kick or power. I quickly emptied a clip into the mound behind the targets and returned to the truck for more bullets. The power was addictive. I felt larger than myself, stronger than I'd ever felt before, and in that moment I came to understand intuitively the strange and overwhelming appeal of guns.

We shot hundreds of rounds, the men switching weapons liberally and then gathering to admire the more powerful ones. We took turns with a particularly nasty shotgun that kicked so hard my shoulder ached for days. Holding it in my hands, I grew in power and stature. I wasn't the kid who used to get bullied. I wasn't the boy who lived in fear. With a gun, a powerful gun, I could be the big, strong man I'd always worried I could never be.

When we were done we returned the guns to their holsters and cases and gathered around the truck once more. The men, my father included, looked exhilarated, their smiles beaming like even they were shocked by how alive they felt. That's how I felt anyway, and when I met eyes with the men we shared glances like we held a secret in common.

There, around the truck, all of us caught in the afterglow, idle chitchat gave way to more pressing matters. I'd caught glimpses of this in the past when my male relatives sat in a room empty of women, in a dingy locker room, and later this setting would be re-created at every Donald Trump rally. The guns had jostled something in them. Studies I'd come across later would explain that handling guns actually increases testosterone in men* and they

---

* Jennifer Klinesmith, Tim Kasser, and Frank McAndrew, "Guns, Testosterone, and Aggression: An Experimental Test of Mediational Hypotheses," *Psychological Science*, August 2006, vol. 17, issue 7.

were definitely more aggressive, and more than willing to voice their opinions. All of their words were soaked with doom. They talked about war, especially the one raging in Iraq, and soon they were liberally exchanging racial slurs, calling Arabs "camel jockeys," "sand niggers," and "towelheads," many of the men wishing they could go overseas and kill some themselves as their eyes lingered over the guns. One fantasized about lining up a bunch of Iraqis, soldiers or citizens, one was just as bad as the other, and seeing how many he could kill with a single bullet.

Their anger wasn't just reserved for Muslims, though. Soon it turned to African Americans who needed to be taught a lesson, and then Mexicans flooding over the border and stealing jobs. Somebody mentioned a group of migrant workers who'd moved into the area and the man next to me laughed and reminisced about the "old days" when the Ku Klux Klan controlled the town and the homes of immigrants would've been set on fire in the middle of the night.

But that wasn't it. They moved onto conspiracies and even though they'd been so keen on slaughtering Muslims for retribution, it seemed agreed upon around the truck that 9/11 had been an inside job, that a group they called the New World Order was behind September 11, as well as getting minorities and women riled up about rights, fixing elections, and even spreading HIV/AIDS, which, one of my dad's friends explained, had been engineered in a lab to reduce the population before the coming apocalyptic battle between good and evil.

I tried not to let on that anything they were saying bothered me, as if their blatant white supremacist and fascist drivel wasn't anything new. It was my youth all over again—I'd gained a measure of acceptance and didn't want to risk it. I was scared, pure and simple, and I didn't have the courage to speak up lest I be ostracized all over again.

Afterward Dad navigated those back roads with only the sound of Alan Jackson fretting over the state of world affairs to keep us company. I wondered if Dad was really like the men back there, or if he'd been like me and frightened into silence, too. The song, which I'd always thought was ridiculous, was about being a simple man meaning well but lost in a new world. Was that how Dad saw himself?

Our fights a few months before over the Iraq War made me wary of discussing politics with him, but something about the guns and the day made me try. I asked if he really believed what those men had been saying.

Dad looked over at me and I'd never seen him so surprised. "No," he admitted, "that's some grade-A bullshit. Tell you the truth, I just never know exactly what to say when they get flappin' their gums like that."

From then on, our relationship fundamentally changed. Something softened in my dad, almost like he'd realized he didn't have to perform an act when we were together, and our conversations around the office were looser and less soaked with dumb posturing and awkward silences. Dad let his guard down and soon he was cracking jokes at his own expense. When he talked politics, his hard-line conservatism lost some of its edge. When I spoke out against the war and the illegal policies of the Bush administration, Dad started to listen and would occasionally nod in agreement and say, "You might be onto something there."

Dad read up on the same issues he'd been so quick to dismiss and became increasingly concerned about the climate and income inequality. To the surprise of his friends at McDonald's, the ones who still wore SEXTON FOR MAYOR hats as they sipped their coffee, he'd point to articles in the paper about the damage of pollution, the dangers of free markets, and the mistreatment of prisoners in Abu Ghraib. Eventually he even traded in his truck for a Prius.

Day by day, he was becoming a different person.

Unfortunately, as my dad was transforming, so was I.

———

The morning after getting caught drunk driving, I woke with a pounding in my head, possessed of a deep and resounding shame. That's how it was so many mornings in graduate school. I forgot what it was like not to have a hangover, not to smell like a smoky bar, not to be racked with guilt and self-loathing.

Any remaining self-pity had dissipated with the alcohol. I came to and saw the rifle lying on the bed next to me and hurried to hide it again. While I did I struggled with the recollection of what had taken place the night before. The run-in with the cop felt like a dream. I played the events over in my head, working back from when I'd blacked out, through being pulled over, to the bar, where I could still recall my friend placing his hand on my shoulder, looking me directly in the eye, and asking if I was all right.

I knew I wasn't. My life was a wreck, a disaster growing worse by the minute. There hadn't been a night in months where I hadn't gotten blackout drunk. I'd alienated myself in my graduate program. I'd lost two partners I cared about because I couldn't stop running around and refused to communicate. I was resoundingly alone, heading nowhere fast.

Sober, it was clear as day. When I wasn't drinking or getting high I knew full well what all my posturing had gotten me. Nothing. Absolutely nothing. Trying to pretend I was some kind of strong man had left me a pathetic mess. I'd hurt my loved ones, put others' lives at risk.

With a little distance now, I can trace the trajectory of my own personal crisis. My upbringing laid the groundwork for my behavior. My experiences as a child had stayed with me and still played a role in determining how I behaved. Though I was rebelling against masculine expectations, I was still subject to them. They defined how I could act and who I could be, especially in uncertain times. When troubled or vulnerable, I reflexively returned to the coping mechanisms of performative gender.

And that's just what happened when I entered graduate school. By that point my persona and years of running around and performing a pale imitation of my father had begun to run its course. I'd slowed down, begun to question the whole act, and even started to write critically about masculinity and what had compelled me to behave as I had. By that first week, I had enough confidence to walk across campus and get to class without the aid of my persona, but I wasn't prepared for what would happen once I got there. In no time at all, I ran afoul of a cruel professor who loved nothing more than to publicly emasculate and humiliate his students, particularly any young man in whom he perceived weakness. I had thought, after years of pretending, that I'd toughened and become invulnerable. All it took was one instance of mortification for that misconception to shatter.

As my tenuous confidence and self-worth were being routinely shredded, I unconsciously regressed to the boorish behavior that had helped me overcome my fears and anxiety, only now it got worse with every passing day. The binge drinking, especially in the presence of my classmates, led me to run myself ragged in an attempt to prove I wasn't the pathetic boy my male role models had portrayed me as being. As Dr. Robb Willer posited in his study of insecure men supporting the Iraq War, self-doubting men are much more likely to overcompensate by behaving in an "extremely masculine way." In essence, men like my graduate-school self begin acting more performatively masculine in an attempt to prove any criticism is off-point.

Again, this is one of the dangers of toxic masculinity. Even a person who works hard to deny its existence or counteract its programming can unwittingly revert to performative gender when challenged. In that moment, I had my identity as a man disputed, and so I fell back into the masculine role I'd learned as a child and then performed as an insecure young adult.

To counteract this crisis, I changed myself wholesale. I started haunting the bars at all hours of the night, and abused my body by consuming as much alcohol as I could get my hands on. Life blurred at the edges. I lost track of time. I took risks that were unnecessary and irresponsible. And then, to further prove I wasn't weak or soft, I transformed my body. As it happened, I couldn't help but remember my stepfather and the boys who'd bullied me about my weight when I was little.

That morning I shuffled into my bathroom at the duplex, stripped off my clothes, and stepped onto the scale I kept in the corner by the shower. When I'd arrived in grad school at Carbondale I weighed 260 pounds. The scale read 163.

For months I'd been rationing my caloric intake. At first it'd started with a restriction to 1,500 calories in concordance with a rigorous workout schedule at the gym. I was shedding pounds at a reasonable pace, but I wasn't happy. As was the case with my drinking, I had a propensity for addiction and so my eating habits followed suit. I cut my caloric intake down to 1,000 calories, a goal that I came in under more days than not, and most of those calories came from beer instead of food. I portioned out snacks that would occasionally trick my body into feeling full even when I'd skipped most meals. And then, I'd make it a point to go to

SIU's recreation center at least once a day, if not twice, where I'd get on a stationary bike for hours at a time and pedal until my legs locked up or I was on the verge of passing out. Going to bed with debilitating hunger gnawing at my stomach became a perverse point of pride.

The routine paid off as I started shedding pounds at an alarming rate. I dropped from an XXL t-shirt to a men's medium, and the physical results helped make up for the emotional pain. Then, my weight loss plateaued. Restricting wasn't enough. To go further I needed to ingest practically nothing but still make it to the gym. I needed to trick my body into thinking I was feeding it, so I started chewing up my food and then spitting it into the trash. Soon, I moved on to making myself throw up my meals.

It never once occurred to me that I was developing an eating disorder. That was something women did. I was showing discipline. I was being strong. Even though my behaviors mirrored those I knew to be disordered eating in women, what I was doing was another thing altogether. The terms "anorexia" and "bulimia" couldn't possibly pertain to a man.

I was wrong, though. According to the Eating Disorders Foundation, 10 million men suffer from eating disorders and are much less likely than women to seek treatment because of the gendered shame. These disorders include anorexia, bulimia, and body dysmorphia, including muscle dysmorphia, sometimes called "bigorexia," in which men perceive themselves as being too skinny and begin bulking up in unhealthy ways.

Nobody was particularly concerned about my weight loss (most people complimented me or told me to keep it up), and I think in part it was because of how inconceivable it was that a man could suffer from eating disorders. But in the midst of my spiral, a professor took one look at me during a meeting and asked if I'd eaten anything that day. I made a dumb casual joke that I'd been eating less but drinking more.

She grimaced. "That's about the most idiotic thing I've heard in forever."

Just like it had in Terre Haute, carrying myself like a red-blooded American man had paid benefits. I'd gotten more dates, more respect, and felt much less insecure and anxious by raising hell and living like there was no tomorrow. My professor's disapproval, though, hit me hard.

But not hard enough to knock me completely out of that cycle. I carried her comment with me for weeks afterward, and it rang in my head that morning after I'd narrowly avoided jail and stood looking at myself in the water-streaked mirror in my bathroom. I looked washed out, scrawny, and like I needed a big breakfast and a month's worth of sleep. Deciding to make a change, I got dressed and walked down the street to a diner I'd liked before my diet consisted of almonds and Miller Lite.

While I ate I made myself a promise. In nearly every other reality I would have been in jail or else out on bail and facing a whole world of shit, but that act of mercy by the officer and my privilege as a white man had given me a chance to make things right. I was going to clean up and get my life together. I was going to start eating and exercising healthily, cut back on the drinking and running around, quit looking to the gun under the bed as an easy option out, and I'd never, ever drink and drive again.

The only resolution I kept was the last one. Never again would I take a chance with my life, or the lives of others, when it came to driving while drunk. But everything else proved harder. Before I went home I stopped by the liquor store to get some beer to celebrate my new lease on life, and I'd downed the first can before I'd gotten the pack in the fridge. Half an hour later, I had my finger down my throat in an attempt to throw up my breakfast. By night-fall I was loading the rifle once more.

———

A year later, I was still in graduate school, and not much had im-proved. I'd moved into an apartment above a doll shop filled with off-putting figurines with creepy glass eyes that seemed to follow you as you walked around the house. I spent all of my free time on the porch out back, where I'd plug in my iPod and listen to outlaw country music while I grilled my dinner and read and drank late into the night, before passing out.

Weekends were particularly hard. I didn't have classes to teach, so I'd stop by a video place on my way home Friday afternoon and rent up to ten movies to have something to fill the hours.

One Friday, my dad called after I'd made my purchase. "Hey," he yelled when I answered, "whatcha getting up to this weekend?"

I looked at the plastic movie cases in disarray across my back-seat. "Not much."

"Well, good. I got tickets to Daytona. I'll be there 'fore you know it."

He hung up then and left me to sit in my car and try to decipher what'd just happened. I tried calling him back to get more infor-mation, but by then he'd stowed his phone away in the glove box of his Prius and was unreachable. Confused, I drove home, got on the computer, and googled "Daytona." The first story that popped up confirmed what I should've already known. That Sunday would be the forty-ninth running of the Daytona 500, NASCAR's biggest race.

Now, it would be hard to properly put into words how im-portant NASCAR was to poor, white, working-class Americans in the first decade of the new millennium. Though in recent years the popularity has waned due to mismanagement, ludicrous rule changes, and a hemorrhaging of the sport's most beloved stars, back then few things united redneck families like "the races." Sundays from February to November were dedicated to gatherings in living rooms where families chatted about drafting strategies, marveled at multi-car pileups, cheered religiously for their favorite drivers, and fluctuated between getting second helpings of that day's homespun supper and dozing off for hundreds of laps at a time.

I've never really been a fan. The races are way, way too long, and there's always been a transparent marketing at work with the advertisers and branding of NASCAR. The sport's roots are in southern bootlegging operations, and the culture surrounding it has always focused on selling masculinity to its viewers with right-leaning celebrities, country artists who'd taken over the genre to be a respite of sorts for conservatives, and a relentless devotion to all things American. To watch a broadcast, particularly in that time period, was to dive deep into the muddled and somewhat frightening subconscious of post-9/11 Middle America.

But I kept tabs on NASCAR for the same reason some atheists still celebrate Christmas. It was something I could talk about with the men in my family, and if you chose to abstain from watching, you were effectively ostracizing yourself from one of the few things that brought people together.

My dad showed up that evening wearing a beat-up Jeff Gordon hat and before he was up the stairs he was already talking pitting strategies and whether it was better to take two or four fresh tires if you were in the lead late in a race.

While I waited for him I'd done a little research and found the drive from Murphysboro, Illinois, to Daytona, Florida, would span roughly nine hundred miles—somewhere in the vicinity of thirteen hours of driving. I'd made a similar trip with Dad when I was younger, but that'd been with the whole family and I'd spent most of the time parked in the backseat with my nose in a book while he knocked back beers and listened to scratchy Willie Nelson cassettes. This pilgrimage to the Daytona International Speedway constituted what would be the longest stretch of time we'd ever spent alone together.

Dad seemed unconcerned.

"What you want to do," he said, leaning against my kitchen counter, "if you're leading the pack, is hope that somebody back there gets in a wreck so you can pit under caution. That way you don't lose your spot."

He paused and looked around at my apartment. Spent beer cans were spilling out of garbage. Every surface was covered in a thick layer of dust. My cranky cat was up on the counter, butting Dad's arm and biting at his Nextel Series zip-up before screaming at him for some attention.

Nodding at the depressing scene, Dad said, "Place could use some light. Maybe open a curtain or two? Wouldn't hurt."

For the first eight hours or so my dad talked about the races he had watched over the years and then turned to Jeff Gordon, one of the more popular and controversial drivers in the entire sport. Gordon had been a departure from the traditional stars, a tiny guy with movie star looks. Some preferred Dale Earnhardt Sr., the "Intimidator," and ridiculed Gordon as being effeminate, while others went even further and spread the consistent rumor that the driver of the #24 car was gay.

"Between you and me," Dad said, "I don't care a lick if Jeff's gay. Let 'im be gay, long as he gets across that finish line faster."

This was a marked difference for Dad. When running for

mayor, I'd watched him argue with a Rusty Wallace fan that Jeff Gordon wasn't a "queerbob," as if the attacks on Gordon had somehow been an assault on his own sexuality, something I'd seen among other fans of Gordon's who'd gotten heckling for his rainbow-colored car and his "fancy hair." But hearing Dad even acknowledge the possibility that Gordon might actually be homosexual—it bears mentioning that Gordon is married to a woman—and that he wouldn't care either way seemed like a huge development.

"Honestly," he said, "I don't care if anyone's gay. What's that got to do with me?"

This flew right in the face of I don't know how many conversations we'd had over the years. Dad was one of the people I'd heard regularly say that gay people were a threat to the fabric of society and argue that it was a choice and a sign of nonexistent morals.

"What's happened with you?" I asked.

We were in Tennessee at that point and Dad was downing one of his customary Diet Sunkists. He worked his tongue in his cheek and took a deep breath before answering. "You know, I've just been doin' a lot of thinkin'."

He started to tell me then about how the time we'd been spending together, particularly since his mayoral bid, had given him a new perspective. The life he'd been living all those years had been one where he'd had to carry himself a certain way lest he got shit from his friends and family. Deep down, the person he was didn't look at all like the one he pretended to be.

"You ever feel like you're wearing a disguise?" he asked.

I told him I did.

"Why'd you feel like you needed all that?"

Hesitating, I said, "I think it was because of you."

I could tell by the look on his face that hit home.

"You know, when I look back, I think it was because of my old man, too. Well, that and maybe I was scared or something."

"Scared of what?"

"I don't know," he said, turning on the blinker and drifting into an exit lane. He'd been pulling into gas stations to go to the bathroom every hour or so, a routine that'd hurt our time getting to Florida and one that he'd dismissed by making fun of himself for having a small bladder. "Feels like I've been runnin' from one thing or another my whole life."

———

Like all races, the Daytona 500 had been fairly boring in the first couple of hours. Cars traded the lead back and forth and with every lap they roared by and then disappeared in the distance. Dad and I and my brother-in-law Brian, who'd driven down separately, watched and hugged ourselves against the unusually brisk Floridian breeze. In the last few laps, however, business picked up and a scramble in the final go-round led to a multi-car pileup right in front of us and one of the closest finishes in Daytona history. When it was all said and done, the track was littered with twisted metal and fire.

Afterward we got in the car and headed back toward the Midwest, Dad and I still excited about the carnage at the racetrack. We played the scene out over and over, Dad wondering if he'd ever seen such a close finish in all his years of watching racing. It took a while to get out of the parking lot, and by that time Dad was desperate to find a bathroom. Back at the raceway he'd gone a suspicious number of times.

I asked if he was feeling okay, but Dad insisted he was fine even though he was pulling off on an exit maybe twenty minutes later to go again. After that, it was roughly every half hour or so, and when he stopped he'd pretend to put some gas in the car, but the meter only showed fifteen to twenty cents at a time.

"I'm fine," he insisted. "Just drank one too many cokes."

I knew better, but I let the matter drop and we listened to some music for a while. After all, it was known in my family not to bother Dad about his health. He'd refused to go to the doctor for decades, even when his hands and feet got to hurting so bad he could barely make a fist or walk from room to room. Then there were the mysterious fluctuations of weight that no one could explain, but Dad wouldn't go talk to someone, no matter how much you got onto him or begged.

A little while down the road, and after a few more stops, he broke the silence and asked what had happened to the girlfriends I'd had, and I admitted to screwing everything up. I was a bad partner. I couldn't communicate, couldn't settle down, couldn't manage to get my life straight. After I'd finished I felt like I'd said too much. Relationships didn't seem like a conversation he'd want to have, much less talking about personal failings or insecurities.

To my surprise, he was game.

"I figure your mom's told you about how things went to shit, huh?" I told him she had and he got a sad grin on his face. "I was a real son of a bitch, Jared. Just a terrible, terrible piece of shit. I couldn't even begin to tell you how much I've thought about all that, what I did, what I didn't do, and I'll tell you the truth, I'll be honest with you right here and right now, there's not a day that goes by where I don't regret it all."

Dad told me the story then about how he'd come home after Mom got him out of the service and how the first thing he'd done was put away all his Marine stuff in a closet, like he was hiding it in shame. Sometimes, when he'd drunk too much, he'd get out his uniform, his dog tags, an old smoke grenade from a training exercise, and turn them over and over in his hands. The way he explained it, there was a hidden John Sexton, and that John Sexton was a coward.

"Your mom didn't hold it against me," he said. "She was just happy to have me home. She didn't want the war, didn't want her husband in Vietnam getting shot at. But I felt . . . I felt—"

"You felt bad."

Dad shook his head. "Bad ain't even the start of it."

According to Dad, he felt like he'd let everyone down, his wife, his mom, his country, and especially his own father. As a kid he'd always felt weak, like he'd failed as a boy and couldn't live up to his dad's expectations, and then, joining the Marines, he thought he'd found the perfect way to put those doubts to rest.

Remembering how afraid he'd gotten as his deployment date crept closer and closer, he said, "I just couldn't do it. I started having these dreams that I was in the jungle. Just running through trees and grass and swamps, something chasing behind me, something or somebody breathing on my neck. I just couldn't handle it."

After he'd come home Dad said he did his best to make the marriage work. But it wasn't enough. In the back of his mind he was a fraud, a coward who had failed at being a man.

To counteract that feeling, he tried to transform himself into a man more like the one he wanted to be. He taught himself how to fix things around the house, to work on the car, to hunt, and all that developed into a fantasy where he and my mom would move to Alaska and live an old-fashioned, rustic life. Maybe if he built a cabin with his bare hands, if he killed and prepared their food, if he could survive in the snowy tundra, he'd finally prove himself.

It was this drive to reinvent himself that destroyed their marriage. Dad was faithful to Mom until he wasn't, that is, until he had the chance. For years he didn't stray, and then he met a group of people who lived a little fast. He felt cool for the first time, and these people had no idea who Dad was and what he had done. That clean slate was attractive. He could play a different role around these people. They knew him as John Sexton, the Marine. He could drink too much. Listen to his music too loud. He could be John Sexton, the Outlaw. He could be the John Sexton who hadn't shied away from the most frightening challenge of his life.

I told him then about my days in Terre Haute and Carbondale, only this time I didn't just brag about my exploits but admitted I'd felt like a fraud, like I was trying to prove something beyond what I was capable of. Then, without thinking, I told him about my eating disorders.

To my surprise, Dad laughed his ass off. "I'll tell you something I ain't told anybody else," he said. "I did the same fucking thing back in the day. I barely ate anything for days and I'd go run for miles, come home, and swallow down a fistful of Dexatrim. That shit used to be fucking speed, man. That was the most messed-up time of my life. I didn't know if I was coming or going, I tell you what."

Dad went off on a rant then talking about men and America and how the two were inextricably linked. This man who'd just years before railed about antiwar protesters being "faggots" and "pussies," myself included, was ranting on how the country had been founded by aristocratic intellectuals who were so insecure about their masculinity that they pretended to be frontiersmen and farmers. He said the reason we got in so many wars was because we were worried about being emasculated.

Referencing George W. Bush, a president he'd quoted and romanticized for years, he said, "Look at that asshole in there now. There's boys dying left and right in Iraq because Junior wants to one-up his dad. You ask me, a shrink could do a hell of a number on W."

We spent the rest of the drive talking about history and politics and how masculinity had plagued both, essentially ruining everything and making life miserable for everyone. Then, not too far outside of Carbondale, a couple dozen bathroom stops in, he got nostalgic and weepy. After all that loneliness, all that misery, all that pretending to be something he never was, Dad said he wished he could go back in time and talk to himself in basic training and let his younger self know he didn't have anything to be ashamed of. Then he said no, he'd rather go back even further, back to when he was just a little boy—"when I didn't know my dick from a hole in the ground," he said—and tell himself to hold his chin up and not worry about what anyone thought.

"'Tween you and me," he said, "I've lost too many years to this shit. I hate what I was, honest to god I do, and getting to talk like this makes me hate it all the more."

Dad pulled into the alley behind my apartment and put the car in park. I got out, grabbed my duffel of clothes from the trunk, and came around to the driver's-side door. He had the window down and his arm hanging over the side, which is how I'll always remember him. I wish now, years removed, that I would've told him that I loved him. I wish I would've told him how big of a relief it'd been to find out that my dad felt the same way I did. But even though we'd just spent hours discussing how awful the trappings of masculinity were, somewhere, deep inside, I was still a prisoner to them. Even though Dad was starting to shake himself free of the influence, I was still as ensnared as ever. I wasn't ready just yet to give up my disguise.

"Thanks, Dad."

"Yeah," he said, a little misty-eyed. "You got it. Talk soon, yeah?"

"Talk soon," I answered, speeding for the door with my keys gripped tight in my fist, the teeth digging into the soft flesh of my palm.

11

After graduate school I was lucky enough to pull down a full-time teaching job at Ball State University in Muncie, Indiana. I was getting paid less than a shift manager at a fast-food place, but at the very least I had a line for my résumé and halfway decent health insurance. I was also in a relationship, a somewhat functional one, and when we moved to Muncie I was hopeful for once. The conversation with my dad had made clear a struggle I'd been having my entire life, and in the months that followed I was able to start trying to be vulnerable again.

The mistake I made was one that I'd made so many times before and would definitely make again. Because I got better, because I got a little perspective, because I was able to wrap my head around the dangers of toxic masculinity, I thought I was cured. As if someone had administered a vaccine, I was free of the disease. Like so many other men, that delusion was at the heart of my problems, and I remained completely unaware that being a decent person was only as easy as living in times that made it easy. When things took a turn for the worst, I relapsed and had to find my way out again.

My optimism soon gave way to cynicism and depression. The salary at my new job wasn't enough to pay for my rent, groceries, and the student loans coming due. For weeks at a time I subsisted on peanut butter sandwiches and whatever was on clearance at the store. Past-due notices started piling up on the counter, and next to them was a crowd of rejections from literary magazines. My career was going nowhere fast, and if that wasn't enough to stoke my worst fears, the world had just suffered an economic meltdown that could possibly result in a depression. Hardly a week went by where I wasn't reminded at work that if push came to shove, my job would be one of the first to disappear.

I turned into a miserable person. There's just no other way to put it. I got irritable, I drank too much, I stewed in my self-pity and returned to my old ways of sitting on the porch, drinking and smoking and listening to despondent music, while my partner tried to pull me out of my funk. There was no saving me, not then anyway, and I drove her away. She fell in love with somebody else, and I was left alone again.

Continuing my self-flagellation, I watched Fox News around the clock. I was still aware that the "Fair and Balanced" network was full of shit, but there was something happening on there that kept me transfixed for hours at a time. This was in the nascent years of the Obama administration, a time where turning on Fox meant tuning in to full-blown hysteria. Anchors reported stories about African Americans and immigrants committing crimes and enjoying special privileges, all the while Glenn Beck connected these stories on a chalkboard with pictures of Barack Obama that made him look like a power-mad tyrant. Every broadcast seemed to tell the same story: something somewhere had gone very wrong.

The rise of the Tea Party in the late aughts synthesized this narrative and put those insecurities into action. The rhetoric of this anti-Obama group centered around taxes and government control, but what you heard when you really listened was that white Americans, particularly white males, felt their grip on power loosening by the day. Their slogans all centered on taking their country back, returning things to the way they used to be, all of it focused on ownership and lost privilege. I grew fascinated with the group and its media coverage because I understood their appeals and recognized the faces in the crowd. They were my people, my family, my loved ones. On social media their memes and messages were creeping into my family's feed, especially my male relatives. I realized the rhetoric was tuned to a special frequency that I, as a frustrated and insecure man, could hear loud and clear. Though my background and my studies inoculated me to the purpose of the rhetoric and kept me from falling into the fold, I could still recognize exactly what tack the Right was taking in trying to reach people like me. Republicans were turning into the party of the aggrieved white male, providing a platform for all the problematic and fascistic opinions I'd been hearing since I was an insecure little boy.

In the summer of 2010 I was visiting home when I read in the paper there'd be a Tea Party meeting at the 4-H fairground outside of town. I'd been watching the growth of the movement from the beginning and had told everyone who would listen how potentially dangerous they were, if only because I understood how they were winning over those closest to me. I wanted to see the danger firsthand.

The event was filled with people I'd known since I was a child stewing in anger and became an out-of-control rage-fest before the speeches about how Barack Obama could be a worse dictator than Hitler and might murder more citizens than Joseph Stalin and Pol Pot combined even began. The conversations in the crowd ran the gamut from quietly prejudiced to full-blown racist. There were slurs against the president, discussions about African Americans who lived on welfare and plotted against white America, fantasies of assassination and full-blown violent revolution. All the recent changes in culture, somebody wearing a star-spangled hat explained, were a result of a giant conspiracy meant to take over the United States.

"You mean the New World Order?" I asked, thinking about the abstract conspiracy theory my relatives and people around town used to talk about.

"You bet," he said. "Obama's in charge of the whole damn thing."

With a start that I realized the paranoid fantasies I'd been hearing the men around me tell my entire life had found purchase in the zeitgeist. Just as we'd all stood around a truck full of guns years earlier, here we were, out in public, discussing international conspiracies meant to inspire racial and societal unrest. Black people were in on it. Immigrants were in on it. Academics like myself were in on it. Even white women were in on it. Everyone, that is, except white men who would either have to stop the plot before it was realized or else die in a blaze of fire defending their homes and families.

"Here," a man sweating through a short-sleeved button-up said as I was about to leave. "Give this a read."

I took a pamphlet he'd obviously printed himself. The colors were off and the text smeared with sweat. "What's this?"

"All of Obama's impeachable offenses," he explained. "You look like the kind of guy who *gets it.*"

I was stunned. I didn't *get it.* I'd sat in horror for hours and hearing all this nonsense out loud had only confirmed my worst fears that something very bad had been loosed with the Tea Party's emergence.

What could he have possibly seen in me that led him to think

I'd ever, ever be a part of that dangerous movement? I stopped by my dad's house for a few minutes and showed him the literature. He looked it over a few times and chuckled nervously. "These people," he said. "I tell you."

Dad told me then that almost all of his friends were starting to talk like Tea Partiers. They were obsessed with Obama; their conspiracy theories were all starting to involve nefarious schemes to get him into power to hurt white men. The talk still sounded like the conversations they used to have, including the one I witnessed at the makeshift gun range, but they were getting worse and more blatant by the day.

"There's a real sickness right now," Dad said. "And it's spreading."

When Dad talked about the movement it was always in reference to disease. In fact, hardly any conversation didn't involve some mention of sickness, and when I brought up the subject to my step-mom Nancy one night she made mention of a secret hiding in plain sight: Dad wasn't well.

You could see it in his difficulty walking. How he grimaced constantly and rubbed his hands as if they were torturing him. He was thin, his arms and legs atrophying. There was something wrong with him.

"How're you feeling?" I asked him that summer day.

"Fine, fine," he said, covered in what looked like a cold sweat. "Fit as a fuckin' fiddle."

I could tell he was lying. Nancy had asked me if I'd try to convince him to see a doctor, a task if ever there was one. "You think maybe you should go talk to someone?" I asked him.

Dad shook his head. He thought he had either arthritis or Lyme disease. Maybe an allergy. Maybe just old age, even though he was only in his fifties. "What about you?" he asked. "You ever think about going to talk to someone?"

Later, I'd stare at myself in the mirror and see that I was look-ing worse for wear again. I had circles under my eyes from where I was burning the midnight oil and running around. I'd lost sig-nificant weight again from restricting my calories and occasionally making myself throw up. It was déjà vu seeing the reflection like that. A bizarre remnant of a past life I'd come to relive.

I told him I was fine, but I was the furthest thing from it.

During the day I'd go teach class, then come home, set up shop on the porch, drink and smoke until I could barely walk, and then come inside to get my gun out of the closet. The routine was old hat by then, and I carried it out as if it were muscle memory. I touched the gun, reminded myself of its realness, its power, and then I'd load the clip with the bullets. This felt normal then. A return to old times. But I was inching up on something else. I'd begun putting the barrel into my mouth, biting the metal with my teeth, and trac-ing the trigger with my finger.

For months I'd been sleeping with my rifle. I'd black out with it, then wake up and be reminded all over again. But, unlike years before, I wouldn't hurry to hide the gun in shame. It lay there on my bed, out in the open, all hours. Now, when I woke up, I wasn't regretting anything. I was looking at the weapon with sober eyes and sober mind and considering ending it all. The choice didn't feel irra-tional. My worries about the grief my loved ones would feel, about leaving behind the world, didn't seem so valid anymore.

———

Winters in Muncie were brutal. Cold and long and filled with ice and banks of snow. They had a tendency to strand you, make you hole up inside alone with everything you'd rather not think about. I'd been isolating myself, collapsing inward, but the short days and ever-present chill took a toll regardless. My depression grew with every creaking step across the wooden floors. I could feel myself withdrawing. I could feel myself giving up.

One night I couldn't bear it anymore. A new round of snow had all but shut down the town and I knew if I didn't get out of the house I wouldn't make it through the night. I layered my shirts and socks, tugged on a pair of boots, donned a coat, and stepped out into a cold that felt like a blanket of needles.

Tromping through mounds of dirty snow, I slowly made my way to a restaurant down the street, where I was the only customer. I settled into a back booth, ordered some food, and asked my server what whiskey they kept. Beaten down and dispirited, I ordered some I couldn't afford and used what little credit I had left to my name. I drank it slowly, never intending to make another payment.

I was sipping my drink and watching the still street and the way the lights shined off the ice when my phone buzzed somewhere in my coat. I didn't need to look to see who was calling. My mom had been checking in constantly as she felt me drifting away. It worked like this: she'd call, make small talk, ask near the end if I was okay, and I'd lie over and over again.

Telling her the truth felt impossible. We'd gone through everything imaginable together, we'd been each other's support through years of abuse, heartbreak, and struggle, but whenever I opened my mouth to tell her how deep of a hole I had dug, to admit I was fraying, the words hitched before they could come out. I'd taken to avoiding her calls altogether rather than continuing to lie to her.

In recent days the debate over killing myself had grown more and more lopsided. Whereas I used to choose to live for the benefit of my mom and the few people who still loved me, I'd started reasoning that I'd become a burden to them. I felt like a rotten weight they'd someday be relieved to no longer bear, even if the initial shock and grief seemed intolerable.

That night, sipping a drink I couldn't afford, I hated myself. Somewhere deep down I knew there was a decent person pinned down by years of delusion and hardening, but he seemed so far out of reach. Back then I'd think often of my life divided between the muck I was mired in and the boy I had been. Even as miserable as I was, even as much as I disliked who I'd become, I still looked back with a tinge of disgust. How had I ever been that boy?

And yet, somehow, I missed him.

Back home, I locked the door and made a drink before putting on a record. The lonely strains of Neil Young's *Harvest* filled the empty rooms. When the first side ended I lifted myself out of my chair and flipped it, then settled in as "Old Man" opened the next movement. It's a haunting song about the legacies of fathers and sons and how we learn self-destruction from those who come before us. Needless to say, it hit home that night and I was inconsolable by the time the first chorus ended. If I was going to end things, and I fully intended to, what better song was there to play when I did it? So, I moved the needle back, started the song over, and retrieved my gun.

I held it, traced it with my fingers, and in that moment I could hear perfectly what that shot would have sounded like. How it would have echoed. And then, with equal measure of shame and morbid humor, it occurred to me how long it would take for anyone to find me. I'd isolated myself so totally there was no one left to worry.

Except my mother, who was still calling. She was the one who kept asking. Already she'd called four times that evening, and I knew, if I was going to go through with it, I needed to say goodbye.

She picked up on the first ring and immediately told me she'd thought something awful had happened. Maybe I'd been in a wreck out there in the storm, maybe something else . . .

"I'm fine," I told her, the loaded gun resting on my lap.

She paused. "Are you? If you weren't, you'd tell me?"

Mom had always leveled with me. She'd been honest about all the trouble we were in. Those days in Owensville when it felt like John might kill us, when she was looking to leave Randy, when Jon was about to go to prison.

"You can talk to me," she said. "You need to talk to somebody."

———

"You know, you're still paying me one way or another."

The therapist had thrown her hands up in exasperation. Over the course of our fifty minutes I'd given her next to nothing. I sat on her couch, picking at my fingernails, answering her questions monosyllabically or else just plain lying, like when she'd asked if I harbored suicidal thoughts and with a blank stare I said no.

"I want you to do something for me," she said, all the nicety gone from her voice. "I want you to go home and, in the next week, I want you to decide whether you want to go another round like this. Decide if you want to just come in and waste my time and yours or if you really want to get better."

I'd followed through on my mom's plea and seen a therapist, but I couldn't shake the shame of having failed to communicate. Here I was, carrying myself like I was some kind of strong man, like I wasn't afraid of anything, and I couldn't tell the truth to a therapist? I'd lied because I was scared, I'd stayed silent because I was scared. Every time she'd asked for some information or insight I'd known exactly what I should have told her, and yet I'd purposefully avoided the hard truth.

The contradiction made me feel like a fraud, and so I drank to quiet my conscience. Eventually, back home, I stumbled into the other room to a bookcase and, fighting my swaying vision, found a book that'd been plaguing me for months.

When my partner had left the previous summer we'd stayed in touch and there was an outside chance of us reconciling, but we could never get past our arguments as to who was to blame. Even as I knew, deep down in my marrow, that I'd been the guilty party, I still couldn't admit it, couldn't let the matter drop. I was too stubborn and proud. The talks went nowhere fast until, one night, she called and gave me an ultimatum: read a book she'd left behind or else we'd never talk again.

The book was this hippy-dippy new-age text about feelings and communication, the kind of thing my ex would read with her discussion groups as they practiced extreme empathy and healthier relationships. I took one look at the cover—a big, bright sunflower holding the planet Earth between its petals—and tossed it across the room. It was too girly, too expressly gendered. Jokingly, I'd told a friend I could feel my testosterone count lowering whenever I saw it lying there on the floor.

But for all my joking, the book terrified me. When I held it my hands would shake and I could hardly read more than a few pages without having to put it down and walk away.

After my appointment, I felt like a coward, so to counteract that I grabbed the book and cracked it open. Even though I was alone, I still made a show of rolling my eyes whenever I came across anything about "getting in touch with my feelings" or "establishing trust." Just like my relatives, I had to pretend to be tough because, in actuality, the concepts were so heavy and frightening that they challenged my identity.

Then, I came across a scenario in the book that hit home. In it, the author was talking to a married couple about their strained relationship, a relationship that was suffering because the wife felt her husband was closed off emotionally. She called him "a wall" and talked about how much it hurt to have a partner maintain such a distance.

Reading that felt worse than any punch in the face I'd ever taken. The example laid bare a contradiction that'd been plaguing me for years. I was trying to be strong so I could survive, so I could be a guardian for the ones I loved, so I could prevent the type of horrors my mom and I had survived. But in doing so I'd inflicted the pain of isolation. In getting harder, or trying to seem hard at least, I'd pushed everyone away and come to hate myself.

Again, in a moment of clarity, I'd come face-to-face with the fact that masculinity was predicated on a lie.

A few days later, I was back on the therapist's couch. The night before I'd laid off my drinking and made a list of things to talk with her about. I'd signed a promise to myself that I wouldn't chicken out, and yet, sitting in my car in the parking lot, I'd nearly bailed on the appointment altogether.

"I want you to look back," the therapist said as I was describing my childhood to her, "and tell me what you see."

"A weak, chubby boy."

"Tell me about him."

I told her about how lonely it'd felt in my family, how all the men had looked at me like I was a freak or lesser than them. I told her about the abuse, the beatings, the insults, the screaming, and the dysfunction. I told her about Pam Foddrill and my mother being stalked and not being able to defend either one of them. I told her about the drinking, the self-abuse.

"When you tell the story," she observed, "it's like there are two of you. That little boy and then the guy sitting here on my couch."

Over the next year we tried our best to reunite the two, the weak, chubby boy and what we came to call The Wall. It turned out that The Wall was something like a suit of armor I'd learned to wear, and I'd worn it until I'd forgotten it was not my own skin. Much like how I'd learned to project authority in the classroom despite not feeling anything like an authority, I'd projected an avatar in the world that embodied all the things I wasn't until it just became who I was. And then, I realized something else: all those years of thinking I was strong enough to not suffer from all the abuse and trauma in my past had been in vain. I'd been suffering from posttraumatic stress and my denial and refusal to seek treatment had only compounded its effects.

With context and therapy, I was able to accept that I wasn't invincible, and when I accepted that, I was able to see how much of my life had been governed and shaped by fear. I'd surrounded myself with worldviews that only fortified my own. I watched movies that reinforced my entitlement. I read books by other white men in order to bolster my narrow perspective. I was actively avoiding everything I considered feminine because it might endanger my ignorance and might, as a result, make me weak.

In one session the therapist told me, "None of those men are watching you anymore. They're not judging you. They're not looking over your shoulder with your every move."

But for years it had felt just like that. Any slipup, whether it was entertaining something gendered or not living up to masculine expectations, just listening to a song someone might consider feminine, felt like it could cause the whole thing to crumble around me. If I was vulnerable, if I faltered, if I was anything besides the stoic, self-assured man, then the façade might evaporate and leave behind the weak, chubby boy to face the world's dangers without any protection.

To my surprise, the exact opposite happened. As I started reading outside the white male canon, I found that the patriarchal voice I'd been afraid of my entire life lost its thunder. I wasn't alone. Others saw the fault in the machinery. The anxiety I'd been carrying and the paradigm strain faded away over time until I finally felt a modicum of freedom. I still carried the responsibility of hard work and empathy, and faced a lifelong struggle to counteract my socialization, but those were small challenges in comparison to lugging the impossible and unachievable burdens of patriarchal masculinity.

Like an addict who gets their addiction under control, I learned to view masculinity as a chronic problem I could never be totally cured of. Every day was a new struggle, as there was no such thing as conquering it. I knew, from previous experience, the easiest thing in the world would be to sink back into those destructive and dangerous behaviors. I'd have moments where I'd stumble, where The Wall would return, but by keeping a constant eye on it and maintaining an awareness that I could always be one disappointment away from falling backward, I was able to at least begin the process of healing.

That road is never easy, however, because America is a bastion of patriarchal pitfalls and consistently reinforces toxic concepts. It's there in our entertainment and in our everyday experiences. You can't turn on the television without watching advertisements or shows designed to appeal to the base instincts of masculinity. You're encouraged to live a "guys will be guys" life with your buddies, purchase a new Harley Davidson and a new wardrobe of leather riding gear in order to simulate the outlaw lifestyle, take out a loan for a giant truck built for a construction site, grab a "Man Card" on your way out the door of the Home Depot, sign up for a monthly "Man Crate" that has to be opened with a crowbar and is filled with barbecue sauces, beard brushes, and hatchets, view one entertainment after another that show men as masters of their own destiny and women as objects to attain, or simply tune into a slate of National Football League games and thus prove that you're tough enough to not care if the players are suffering brain damage.

In our families, workplaces, and friend groups we're inundated with socialization and pressure to conform. With men, talk among themselves often drifts into offensive territory, like the now-infamous "locker room talk," in which each member of the conversation tries to outdo one another in terms of harshness and, knowingly or unwittingly, reinforces misogynistic worldviews and perpetuates rape culture. At home, we oftentimes watch passively as traditional gender roles play out and our friends' wives are relegated to chores and the kitchen or their sons and daughters are treated differently and unfairly.

Society and culture have been molded to fit the whims of men and perpetuate the lie of gender, and it requires constant work and exhaustive effort to look between the lines and understand the energies that influence behavior. Beginning to tackle my own shortcomings was a start, but the fight's never over because, for men, it's the simplest thing in the world to sit back and watch the patriarchy work in your favor. That privilege is strong and to our benefit, but it comes with great cost. It harms ourselves and the people we love, holds society back from its true potential, and, in many cases, destroys us.

In so many cases, I'd made terrible mistakes in how I approached masculinity. I thought I controlled it even while it wrested from me any and all control. Similarly, I had made the mistake of thinking it was my decision whether my life continued or came to a premature end. With my finger on the trigger of my gun, it was my choice to make, my course to chart. Like so many men, I considered that agency part of my birthright, and never stopped to wonder if the habitual abuse I'd heaped on my body could somehow tip the scales. It never occurred to me that living like a man would mean dying like a man.

12

The call came in the middle of the night and when I hung up I lingered in bed, confused as to whether I was still asleep or if I'd dreamed the conversation entirely. Nothing about it made sense. Not the hour of the call or my stepsister's calm voice as she delivered the news that my dad had been rushed to the hospital.

I threw on a pair of jeans and the warmest clothes within arm's reach, but on the drive I rolled down the window to let the November cold help wake me up. I'd made it halfway to Indianapolis before I realized I wasn't still entrenched in a dream. The puzzle pieces started to lock in place. As I walked into the hospital, I steeled myself in an effort to be a pillar for my family. To help, I tried to summon the old persona I'd been able to shed with therapy. When I entered the room I wanted to project an air of confidence, of capability. I wanted to reassure everyone that things were going to be all right. Then, through the glass walls of the ICU, I saw him, my father, helpless.

In thirty years I'd only seen Dad sick a handful of times, but he was always there in his dental lab from morning to night. He still went out, mowed the yard, and worked on the house or in the garage. Now I found him in a completely alien state: incapacitated and frail.

Later, in the waiting room, Nancy told me the truth. For years Dad had been in agony and going out of his way to hide it from everyone. Because he hurt so bad he didn't want to make the trek into bed and had been sleeping in a chair in the living room. He'd stopped showering but maybe once a week. That night he'd gotten mean because she'd noticed he was obviously in extraordinary pain and wanted to call for help. When she went to touch him he'd screamed at her, and then she'd seen that he'd urinated on himself.

Nancy shook her head as she filled me in on Dad's secret. She was sure that by not going to the doctor for decades he'd damned himself to a premature death. He was only fifty-nine years old and already he'd begun wasting away.

"I don't know what to say," she told me, "but your father is a proud man. Proud to the point of killing himself."

———

According to a recent study by the Centers for Disease Control and Prevention, American men's life expectancies are dropping while others' increase, leading the divide between male and female life expectancy in this country to grow to five years. Women are now expected to live to eighty-one, while men's expectancies have declined for the past two years. Men's deaths now come at such a clip that they've actually affected the American average because of so-called "despair deaths," or deaths resulting from suicide, addiction, and a rise in diabetes, which ultimately took my father's life.*

To begin looking for an answer as to why men die earlier than women, I asked my friends, relatives, and acquaintances why they thought, in a society built in their favor, men live shorter lives.

Answers I received spanned from sarcastic to deathly serious. One man laughed as he said men died younger because "women nag them to death." Another cited his own father, who, after decades of arduous labor, fully expected to die before he reached retirement, explaining, "He's just completely and totally used up."

Traditionally men have occupied jobs more physically intensive than women. Since his release from prison my stepfather Jon has toiled in a factory and he can barely get out of bed some mornings. The kind of outlaw behavior he and my father engaged in in their earlier years also plays a role. Men are statistically more likely to take risks and put their own well-being in jeopardy, mostly to prove they aren't afraid of the consequences. This accounts for any number of deaths resulting from accidents and addictions, not to mention the high rate of men who die by suicide or homicide.

A few answers revolved around the same issue that led to my own father's premature death: men's refusal to go to the doctor.

Here, the numbers are overwhelming. In comparison to women, men are half as likely to go for a semiannual checkup with a doctor.† In interviews, men have responded that only 12

---

* Olga Khazan, "Middle-Aged White Americans Are Dying of Despair," *The Atlantic*, November 2015, theatlantic.com/health/archive/2015/11/boomers -deaths-pnas/413971.

† "Summary Health Statistics, National Health Interview Study, 2014," Centers for Disease Control and Prevention, ftp.cdc.gov/pub/Health_Statistics /NCHS/NHIS/SHS/2014_SHS_Table_A-18.pdf.

percent of them consult a doctor first when a medical issue arises, only 61 percent seek medical attention when a problem becomes "unbearable," and only 42 percent seek treatment when they realize they have a serious medical issue. Like my father, men are compounding problems that could be treated and/or avoided if only they'd sought timely assistance. They're letting cancers, chronic issues, and festering illnesses like diabetes and heart problems grow worse with every passing day.

Even though I watched my own father die because of his reticence, in this regard I'm still guilty. When I get sick I try to grin and bear it without so much as taking ibuprofen or over-the-counter medicines. Multiple times now I've avoided tackling a serious illness I knew I should've seen an expert about until it became debilitating. I've had hospital stays and been carried out on a stretcher because I was too stubborn to make an appointment or walk into a clinic. Even now, as I write this very sentence, I'm struggling with serious health problems that could have been easily avoided if only I'd sought help sooner.

Personally, my reasons are a mixture of pride and fear. I want to be stronger than illness and let my immune system fight it out rather than admit I'm vulnerable. This is completely absurd, but so are most of the actions of performative masculinity. There's also another factor: I'm terrified of what might happen if I subject myself to a battery of tests and scrutiny. Regularly I have nightmares that I'll go in for a routine physical and end up admitted into an ICU like my father, where my body will be prodded and broken, eventually littered with tubes and dependent on machines.

After my father's ordeal you'd think I'd feel differently, but somehow his experience only fortified my view on doctors. When I get sick, when I get injured, when I think that something has gone awry, I suffer silently with anxiety and worry until it either relieves itself or gets so bad the decision is taken out of my hands.

This is a common fear with men, who say time and again one of the main reasons they avoid doctors is the possibility of bad news. Everyone I interviewed admitted they were terrified of a test uncovering something life-threatening, and instead of facing the potential illness head-on and preventing it from worsening, men like myself are, as Seidler explains in *Unreasonable Men*, ". . . threatened by what our bodies might reveal to us, for they might reveal a weakness that can compromise our masculinity."

That possibility lays the groundwork for an interesting conclusion much of this book has been tiptoeing around. In all facets men have actively overcompensated for their insecurities, so much so that they have endangered themselves, the people they love, and their society as a whole. They've built and reinforced a vast and hidden system of dominance over generations, a system that has actively discriminated against women and anyone who doesn't look or behave like them. Now, in an era of change and perceived crisis, they've doubled down on poisonous masculinity that hurts every single person it encounters.

But why?

Obviously men are so petrified by fear of emasculation and looking weak that they'll overcompensate until they become parodies and literally endanger themselves. They're so unsettled by women living their own lives or thinking their own thoughts they'll manipulate them financially and socially or intimidate them with threats or actual violence. And they're so fearful of appearing weak or facing a challenge that they're willing to live shorter, more miserable lives.

What is it, I keep asking myself, that we're so afraid of?

———

The open-heart surgery felt like the end. The surgeon and nurses had been blunt in their assessment when they told us they weren't sure if Dad could make it through the procedure. We filed in two at a time to say our goodbyes and then held each other as we wept in the waiting room. The day after, as the rest of my family huddled around his bed, a nurse whispered to me in the hallway that it'd been a miracle he'd survived.

On the other side lay a small glimmer of hope. We'd been told Dad's situation was grave, that his condition was deteriorating, but he'd proven them wrong. He was Dad, after all. There was nothing he couldn't take on and best. There was nothing he couldn't fight his way through.

For a while it seemed like he'd turned a corner. When he wasn't on a respirator he chatted with us, watched basketball games on the tiny television on the wall, and cracked some bad jokes like in the old days. Some nights I'd leave his room convinced he was bound to make one of the most astonishing recoveries in the history of modern medicine. You heard stories all the time about people who'd beaten the odds and overcome grim prognoses. Why not him?

Those glimpses of hope were short-lived, as moments of stark reality shattered the illusion. Like when a nurse would come in to change his sheets and you'd get a glimpse at his legs, which had withered into thin sticks of bone. Or, when they'd lift him off the bed like a helpless infant. You could see it in his eyes that every remnant of the powerful man we'd once known was gone. He'd been reduced to a frightened child who cried when he thought people were leaving him. He grew shamelessly afraid of the dark and talked about his fear of death, a subject I'd heard him scoff at for decades.

Eventually Dad was moved out of the Indianapolis hospital and shuffled through the system. The transfers were grim and took a toll as he landed in an overcrowded nursing home where the halls were filled with the wailings and cries of lonely and anxious patients.

His roommate was a young man who'd been paralyzed in a car crash and whose mother watched over and doted on him like a newborn. I thought maybe I'd visit and set up the TV so Dad and I could watch some basketball. It took an hour to get a game on the screen, and by then Dad was sweating through his sheets and whispering desperately for me to ring a nurse. I sat and waited with him for an hour and a half, trying to manufacture some of that small talk we'd always busied ourselves with, discussions about everything but what mattered, the best offenses and defenses, whether this coach was better than that one, and who was the best player Dad had ever seen, the kinds of things Dad would go on about for hours at a time if you let him. But he was in such grueling pain he couldn't get past it. By the time the nurse arrived to change Dad and put him to bed, I'd already turned off the television.

On the way to my car I was in such a hurry that I tripped over my own feet and fell hard enough to bloody my knees. There, on the ground, I vomited into the dusty gravel as I realized the miracle had been fleeting. There wasn't going to be a recovery.

I was watching my father die.

————

This past April I was put on the shelf with a case of bronchitis that, once it got its hooks in me, wasn't eager to let go. It spanned the entire month and leaked into May, which was when I finally got to the point where I could go about my day without having to brace myself against a wall while I caught my breath or get more than a few minutes of sleep without waking up in agony. Later on in my torment one of my colleagues asked if I was still sick and then wondered if I had a case of the "man flu."

I'd never heard the phrase before, and after I'd gotten home and downed some emergency DayQuil, I gave it a search. Apparently it'd been a longtime joke that when men got sick they would exaggerate their illness and symptoms, or rather, that men were much more likely to whine when ill. In the past I'd heard the women in my family joke about it, saying, "You know how men are," which was confusing. If men were so tough, why did they suffer more in this particular instance?

Curious, I looked deeper and found a cache of research that would change how I viewed men forever.

It turns out the pejorative phrase "man flu" has a basis in reality, as men actually suffer from weaker immune systems than women.* In fact, studies have shown that higher levels of testosterone could fundamentally weaken immune functions.† And once you enter the world of biological differences between the sexes, the entire societal construct of the patriarchy and toxic masculinity suddenly take new shape.

To begin, it's important to look at the distribution of sexes upon birth, a number that has always lingered around 106 male births for

---

* Kyle Sue, "The Science Behind 'Man Flu,'" *BMJ*, December 2017, www.bmj .com/content/359/bmj.j5560.

† Mark Davis, "In Men, High Testosterone Can Mean Weakened Immune Response, Study Finds," *Stanford Medicine News Center*, December 2013, med .stanford.edu/news/all-news/2013/12/in-men-high-testosterone-can-mean -weakened-immune-response-study-finds.html.

every 100 female.* That ratio has been mostly consistent through time, and the reason for the imbalance has to do with the discrepancies between men's and women's abilities to survive. As Dr. Marianne J. Legato, founder of Columbia University's Partnership for Gender-Specific Medicine, lays out in her book *Why Men Die First*, ". . . men from conception until death, are inherently more fragile and vulnerable than women. In virtually every society in the world, men die first. Women have a hardiness that men simply don't possess." Dr. Legato goes so far as to call men biological "underdogs," citing that they are "six weeks behind in developmental maturity at birth," have "four times the developmental disabilities," and "suffer more severely than women from seven of the ten most common infections that humans experience . . ."

The uphill biological battle men face starts in the womb, where, before sex differentiation, all embryos begin as female. With men there is leftover evidence of this fact as we are born with nipples and the raphe line in our scrotums, which is where our vaginas would've developed had we continued our trek into being born female. The transformation into maleness is more complicated and leaves us vulnerable to difficulties and outside factors, like environmental pollutants, and this vulnerability has been cited by scientists as contributing to any number of problems men suffer in greater number, including premature birth, autism, and childhood asthma.†

If that weren't bad enough, from the start men are at a tremendous biological disadvantage. Women with their XX chromosomes

---

* David Steinsaltz, J. W. Stubblefield, and J. E. Zuckerman, "The Gender Mystery Starts Nine Months Before Birth," *Nautilus*, August 2015, nautil.us /issue/27/dark-matter/this-gender-mystery-starts-nine-months-before-birth.
† Alice Shabecoff, "Are Men the Weaker Sex?" *Scientific American*, February 2014, scientificamerican.com/article/are-men-the-weaker-sex.

enjoy a benefit in that their twin chromosomes protect them from diseases and can, in the case of one of the chromosomes suffering a defect, effectively serve as a backup copy to supplement the problem.* In terms of evolutionary biology, it's beginning to appear in studies that even viruses tend to favor women as they serve as better hosts while men, on the other hand, are more likely to suffer or be killed.†

As Dr. Legato put it, in almost every facet it seems like women are possessed of "hardiness" that men are not. Or, as Dr. Steven Austad, chair of the biology department of the University of Alabama at Birmingham, remarked, in all of his research he had "found that women had resistance to almost all the major causes of death" and that "humans are the only species in which one sex is known to have a ubiquitous survival advantage." One study after another has proven women enjoy advantages that make them less susceptible to diseases and live longer lives, whether it's through biological or environmental means.

But what does that mean for men?

I can't help but think again of the anecdote from Dr. Cordelia Fine's *Delusions of Gender*, of all those male infants crying more than their female counterparts. All those babies who haven't been subjected to socialization, to unreasonable societal expectations. All those little boys born more fragile and more vulnerable than the girls around them.

---

* Arthur P. Arnold, Karen Reue, Mansoureh Eghbali, Eric Vilain, Xugi Chen, Negar Gharhramani, Yuichiro Itoh, Jingyuan Li, Jenny C. Link, Tuck Ngun, and Shayna M. Williams-Burris, "The Importance of Having Two X Chromosomes," *Philosophical Transactions B*, February 2016, vol. 371, issue 1, 688.
† Sam Wong, "Viruses May Have Evolved to Hit Men Hard but Go Easy on Women," *New Scientist*, December 2016, newscientist.com/article/2115987 -viruses-may-have-evolved-to-hit-men-hard-but-go-easy-on-women.

Just as Dr. Marilyn French asserted in her essay "Power/Sex" that men were driven to create an artificial gendered identity because they lacked one and women naturally held a biological purpose as mothers, could it be that the patriarchy, with all of its abuses and injustices, was created to overcompensate for the fact that men, despite their bluster and beating of their chests, are inherently weaker than women?

———

Holidays in hospitals are surreal. At Christmas the halls are decked merrily, you might come across a man playing Santa Claus in the elevator on your way to see your dying father, and lights twinkle when the lonely and depressing night settles in. Sometimes it's hard to reconcile the envisioned happiness the holidays are supposed to bring while someone you care about suffers in a clinical, impersonal setting. The morning I'd come to have an important talk with my incapacitated father was the day after Valentine's Day and bright red heart stickers still adorned every free surface and paper cupids dangled from the ceiling tiles by lengths of string. On Dad's door someone had taped a card reading ALL YOU NEED IS LOVE.

Normally it was the kind of stuff Dad would've hated. I'd never heard him talk about love. Never heard him say I love you to anyone. In fact, I'd never heard him say he loved anything, person or otherwise. It was girly stuff, unbecoming of a man, and on my way in I nearly took the card down because it felt so antithetical to who my father was as a person.

But he wasn't the same. The procedures and all the moves had ravaged him. He was unable to lift his arms, confined permanently to a bed. When he wasn't on a respirator he could only sustain himself for a few minutes at a time, and that was on a good day. Months had passed before I finally came around to the fact that this wasn't going to have a storybook ending. Dad wasn't going to wake up one morning and spring out of bed. There weren't going to be family dinners where we all gathered around a table and marveled at how far he'd come. For Dad's remaining days, however few were left, he'd be bedridden and totally dependent on machines and medical supervision.

I'd come to talk to him about exactly that. The night before I'd gotten a phone call from Georgia Southern University offering me a tenure-track position as a professor of creative writing. In my field there are very few of these jobs in the country and they're incredibly competitive. The job would double my salary, meaning I'd finally be able to make a decent living and begin my career in earnest. Exactly 744 miles separated my father's hospital bed and Statesboro, Georgia, though. There'd never be a time Dad could make that trip. He wasn't capable of getting in a car and driving down on a random Friday night when the urge hit him. And I'd only be able to visit when I came home for the holidays or in the summer.

Conflicted doesn't even begin to describe how I felt. I had worked so hard to get to the point where I could land a tenure-track job and yet the offer had made me break down and weep the night before. When I went to Statesboro for the campus interview, I spent the night in my hotel bundled under the covers in the fetal position and staring blankly at the wall. I couldn't help but feel like I was betraying my father and leaving him to die.

Before I gave my decision I needed to talk with him, so I made the trek down to Indianapolis, where he'd been moved since his condition had worsened, and was relieved to find him alone. When I walked in the door he was asleep, so I took a seat beside him and held his hand for a half hour or so. Dad and I had avoided physical touch for years, but since his illness I'd found those past barriers fell by the wayside.

He came to and said hello with his eyes. Over time, with the respirator, he got to a point where he could communicate with just a look or two and you knew instantly whether it'd been a decent day or a rough one, whether he was hopeful or scared. That morning, as I tried to catch him up on what was going on around the world, in politics and sports, he was exhausted, and he gave me a look that said he knew something was wrong.

I started to tell him about the job when a nurse walked in with a clipboard. Like most of the people who took care of Dad, we'd talked a few times, and she asked me how I'd been as she checked his vitals. Dad caught her attention and let her know with his eyes he wanted to be taken off his respirator so we could talk. The nurse did as he asked, but instead of letting us have some time alone, she handed me a suction tool I'd seen other nurses use to clean Dad's mouth and asked, "You probably know how to use this by now, yeah?"

I held the device in my hand as a few tears streamed down my face and nestled into my beard. "No," I admitted.

The nurse gave me a quick tutorial and then returned to her checklist, leaving me with the chore of cleaning my paralyzed father's mouth. Dad seemed utterly humiliated, but then I did what came natural. I reached out with my fingers and brushed his downy hair from his forehead. The strain of not being on the machine taxed him and large drops of perspiration were already beading up on his skin.

Like a parent reassuring their child, I told him, "It's okay. It's really okay."

Dad cried then and said thank you as I kept caressing his hair and using the suction tool like the nurse had instructed me. When I was done she took the device and left the room. I was still standing over him, touching his hair. I don't think I ever cried in front of him like I did that day. I'd always been afraid to, and even as I did I felt so worried he would think less of me or reprimand me, but then he was crying just as hard. There were no signs of his armor anymore.

I told him that I'd gotten the job and what taking it entailed. That I would be three states away and would rarely see him. I told him I was sorry that I couldn't get a job closer to home, that if he wanted I would turn it down and keep trying to find something in Indiana.

He stopped me then, his voice quieter than a whisper as he told me I had to take the job. He said he knew I worked hard and that he was as proud of me as he could be. I was sobbing and barely heard what he said next, but luckily he repeated it over and over. He told me he loved me. It was the first time I'd ever heard it.

Soon after I had to ring the emergency call button because the strain was too much. Dad needed the machine. I stayed there with him until he fell asleep, holding his hand, touching his hair, telling him I loved him, too, and gazing mournfully into the hallway, where the nurses' station was located. Around it were gathered the women who watched over my dad, who changed him when he soiled himself, fed him his meals, carried him, and addressed his every need. They were checking charts or else hurrying to their next patient. Everywhere I looked were women doing the heavy work for men who needed them desperately and without fail.

———

Dad died April 15, 2012. Tax Day. Again, the call came from my stepsister. She was shaken but relayed all the necessary information. I hung up and walked down the street to a nearby bar and proceeded to get as drunk as I ever had. At one point the guy sitting next to me said something I didn't care for and I tried to start a fight. What I wanted right then was to either hurt somebody or have somebody hurt me. We ended up outside, but he took pity on me as I could barely stand.

The next morning I dragged myself out of bed and drove to Linton. I was in a state of shock. I'd watched Dad die a little day by day. John Sexton seemed bigger than death, though. Remembering all the dumb legends about him, the idea of his actually dying felt ludicrous.

That night I walked downtown to a place where Dad had always hung out, a hole in the wall called Sportsman's Pub. They'd gotten to know me over the years, and whenever I came in the bartender would tell me about the good ol' days when Dad and his buddies would come in after their bowling league and tie one on. There were still trophies lining the wall from those years, my dad's name inscribed on the plaques.

I sat there until last call and jotted down some thoughts in a little notebook. I was going to give Dad's eulogy and it hadn't occurred to me until then that to do so I was going to have to untangle his life and try to come to some kind of peace with our relationship. The conversations I'd been having since getting home, including the ongoing one with the bartender who lionized my father even as I wrote his eulogy, were all about how great of a man Dad was.

That was the phrase.

"Great man."

When people used it they were always referencing his utility, what he did for them, what chores and physical activities he carried out, how he'd been so strong and resolute.

Something didn't sit right with me. That man, that reckless, hell-raising man's man, was the same guy who had ignored me for the majority of my life. He'd kept Nancy, and my mom before her, waiting up all hours of the night, wondering where he was and whether he'd killed himself by acting irresponsibly or driving drunk. He'd made my stepbrother and me question our worth as men. He'd been distant, unreachable, at times brutal, the exact opposite of who he'd shown himself to be in the years leading up to his illness and his eventual decline.

The day of his funeral I put on a black suit and steeled myself. Again, I needed to affect an air of strength just to make it through the day. My legs were tired, my stomach churning. I shook the hands of distant relatives I'd never met before and all the running buddies who made cameos in Dad's stories. To a person they told me how much I'd come to look like my father and how great of a man he'd been.

I walked up to the pulpit unsure if I'd give the eulogy I'd written. Sitting at Sportsman's I'd composed a remembrance that toed the line between reality and myth, that painted a complicated portrait befitting someone like Dad. But then, standing in front of the bereft, after hearing their stories, their own memories of him, I worried any attempt to do so would not only fall flat but soil the fantasy he'd worked so hard to create for so many years.

Fumbling with my notes, I took a steadying breath and came to a decision. What made it for me was that conversation we'd had driving back from Florida. Dad had been ashamed of his mythology, regretful that he'd spent so many years running from himself and hurting others in the process. There was no comparing the man he'd become and the man he'd left behind, and so, that day, I buried them both.

At long last I tried to reunite the two, the sensitive boy punished by his overbearing father and the troublemaker who raged late into the night, the angry young man who was a danger to everyone and the frightened child in a hospital bed. I tried to tell the story of a man who could be careless and cruel at moments and tender and thoughtful the next. I wanted them to see how this contradiction could come to pass, how a boy could come into this world with the best of intentions and somehow get so very lost. I needed them to know the buddy they'd run around with, the cousin they'd known, the stepfather they'd looked up to, the husband they'd stood beside, had finally come around, that the years of coldness and distance had mercifully given way.

I needed them to know about the boy who would sacrifice all his toys to anyone willing to be his friend, the boy who'd been locked away nearly his entire life, but who sprung loose in those final years—vulnerable and terrified, yes—but above all, finally, free.

III

A CRISIS OF OUR OWN MAKING

13

In the spring of 2015, three years after I'd buried my father and moved to Georgia, I was restless and looking for a hobby. Intrigued by the upcoming presidential election, I decided to throw myself full-force into the contest the way some people do with a sport or pastime. My plan was to analyze the many ups and downs of the 2016 election, write a few pieces, and eventually make my way to some events and rallies.

As anyone who's covered politics can tell you, it gets addictive. In fact, the great Hunter S. Thompson regularly described journalists as "junkies" who can never give up their fix. If you're in the right place at the right time, you can feel history rushing past you like a river flowing over stones. What began as a hobby and a distraction became an obsession, and soon I was lighting off for Iowa to get a close-up view of what I'd been watching from afar.

Out west, I spent a week attending rallies for Martin O'Malley, Chris Christie, Bernie Sanders, and then Hillary Clinton, spending my nights in cheap hotels and chatting with locals and political operatives. It was like catching a glimpse behind the curtain. There was what we saw on television, what played out in prime-time, and then the operation behind the scenes that sought to influence the show.

A few days later Dylann Roof killed nine parishioners of Charleston's Emanuel AME Church. The tragedy captivated the country, and I felt drawn to Charleston. Before heading to Mother Emanuel, though, I visited Roof's home in Eastover. The area featured the few fast-food restaurants every town now seems to have, a National Guard base, and not much else to speak of. As I ventured around I was struck by how depressed everyone seemed. I saw plenty of guys who looked just like the men back in Linton, many of them drinking though it was early in the afternoon.

The attack in Charleston prompted a brief national debate on guns that pivoted to the Confederate flag, which Roof had been pictured with multiple times. As pressure began to mount over the symbol, there were several black churches set on fire in the South. I drove from one decimated house of worship to another and found the areas teeming with more Confederate symbols, as well as frequent scrawlings of swastikas and hate speech. There seemed, at that moment, to be something incredibly ugly and dangerous starting to seep out from under the country's veneer.

Up until then Donald Trump's candidacy had been treated more as a sideshow than a viable campaign, and because the spectacle earned big ratings, the major networks aired his speeches around the clock. In the beginning, Trump would take to a podium and all coverage would stop as cameras were pointed in his direction to capture whatever drivel came out of his mouth.

There didn't seem to be even a slight chance for Trump to win the Republican nomination, much less the presidency. The professionals and journalists I talked to mostly predicted he'd bow out after a poor showing in the Iowa caucuses and sulk back to NBC and his *Celebrity Apprentice* reality show. Members of the campaign itself told me later they all expected Trump to cash in on his support and start an alternative to Fox News.

But then, of course, everything changed.

―――――

By the time I attended Senator Tim Scott's Q&A with Trump in September 2015, the Confederate flag hadn't flown over South Carolina's state house grounds for two months, but the decision remained a contentious subject for the Columbia crowd, who blamed Governor Nikki Haley, social justice activists, minorities, and Republicans who had capitulated in the controversy. Outside there were heated debates over political correctness, or, as it was referred to, the "pussification" of the country, and tense arguments about "illegals" and other ungrateful minorities. The audience was filled to the rafters with white men loudly voicing their anger.

Trump's appeal was based in his ability to mimic that anger and then, once he'd assured them he was as angry as they were, to give them a direction in which to channel it. During the initial speech announcing his candidacy, he'd immediately singled out Mexicans with his now-infamous charge that Mexico wasn't "sending their best," that the immigrants who were coming were bringing drugs and crime with them, as well as the threat of rape. Later, on the heels of terrorist attacks in Europe, Trump extended his target by calling for a ban on immigration from Muslim-majority countries.

I was there that night aboard the USS *Yorktown* in Mount Pleasant and waited in line with Trump supporters chatting about the dangers of letting immigrants into the country and minorities who threatened the safety of their families. They loved that Trump was holding the event on an aircraft carrier, relieved to have a "strong" man to look up to after eight years of a president they considered a wimp. Inside the crowd reflected back to Trump his burning rage and roared as he announced the proposed ban. When protesters interrupted the speech, supporters would surround them and attempt to intimidate them into silence.

After walking off the USS *Yorktown*, I came face-to-face with a protest consisting of younger people chanting that Trump was racist. There was a division between them and the Trump supporters who filtered in to oppose them, a group made up entirely of young white men who called the protesters "pussies" and "faggots" and threatened them with violence, a scene that would replay itself at every Trump rally thereafter. A subgroup of supporters, eyes narrowed and hands squeezed into fists, talked about wanting to "crack some fucking skulls" and how badly they wanted to beat the protesters. I heard several people threaten to shoot them, and another man joked to me that he'd like to use a commemorative turret gun to mow down every last one in cold blood.

One man stepped into the gap dividing the two groups that'd been established by the police and lobbed a wild haymaker through the air. Screaming so hard his voice broke, he threatened to fight every single protester and continued to challenge them until an officer returned him to his side of the street. It was a physicality and posture reminiscent of what I'd seen growing up and reminded me of how men could turn to violence at a moment's notice. Right then it dawned on me that something fundamentally connected that mindset to the campaign Trump was waging.

"Do you hear what they're saying, man?" he yelled just a few inches from my face after he noticed I wasn't chanting "All lives matter" with the rest of the Trump supporters. "Black lives matter? Are you going to let them get away with that?"

Just like the lead-up to a bar fight, it was an ultimatum. You either backed down or you let your pride lead you into a brawl. I stepped away and watched from afar as the confrontation continued.

As the protesters were led away, people driving by threw trash at them and leaned out their windows to make threats and shout homophobic slurs. I couldn't believe what I was watching, and I couldn't believe that I'd been able to go into a rally with these people without being immediately identified as an intruder.

———

Over the next year I'd slip into Trump events around the country, becoming privy to undisguised conversations as the people having them had no reason to suspect I didn't share their opinions because I looked like them, dressed like them, and, just as I'd found whenever I'd slipped on my persona as a rough-and-tumble man, they believed I *was* one of them. Years earlier it'd been around the bed of a truck containing mounds of weapons; now it was in arenas and auditoriums decked out in star-spangled bunting. I carried the markers of a working-class white male, and so I was allowed the unembellished truth and given access to men talking like men.

Unguarded, they talked about women's not knowing their place, particularly women like Hillary Clinton, whom they regularly fantasized about hanging, murdering, raping, or attacking. Women like Hillary were "cunts," "bitches," and "dykes" determined to ruin everything. On the subject of minorities, they maintained that blacks didn't know how good they had it, some arguing that slaves were actually treated well, and that Mexicans were lazy criminals who knew just how to bilk hardworking Americans out of their tax dollars. They wondered aloud what it was going to take to re-claim their country and their birthright, be it violence, murders, or revolution.

At its core, the Trump phenomenon was a movement a long time in the making. The frustrations my family and the men around me had been feeling for decades finally metastasized into a political identity that went beyond Democrat or Republican as both par-ties had lost purchase. Democrats were blamed for focusing on the rights of "the other," meaning women and minorities, and Republi-cans had exhausted their political capital after years of promises to "real Americans" who still hadn't seen benefit from their policies.

Trump's telling them they couldn't trust the Republican Party cemented his status for this bloc of voters as someone who "tells it like it is," a masculine designation they'd first bestowed upon him after his announcement. In that address, which most experts thought would be the end of his candidacy before it ever began, men saw in Trump a realist who wasn't going to kowtow to political correctness, which had already been effectively gendered as female. They saw themselves in this exact same way. They were the ones who owned reality and it was the others around them looking to subvert it. This meant that women's looking for equality, minorities' beginning to share in America's wealth, and the changing emphasis of the economy from labor and industry to creative and educated careers were all signs of a culture being overrun by anti-masculine forces.

At every opportunity Trump echoed this worldview. He em-braced language that divided the world between winners and los-ers, the United States having fallen into the latter category because of the "pussification" so many supporters decried. Obviously the country was becoming more feminine if we weren't as worried about competition, however that might be defined, and if we were suddenly moving toward empathy, which was a highly gendered mindset. Trump espoused toughness, both in philosophy and action, turned empathy into a laughing matter, proved his toughness through cruelty, and gave no credence to "feminine" issues like climate change or the social safety net. He said he wanted to personally hit protesters, waxed nostalgically about the days when those who opposed him would be wheeled out on stretchers, and even criticized the military for being weak, citing our distaste for torture and war crimes.

On the subject of torture, Trump painted the Obama administration's decision to cease waterboarding enemy combatants as weak, saying "Torture works" and "we should go much stronger than waterboarding."* Trump regularly told the apocryphal story of John Pershing, a World War I general who supposedly lined up Muslim dissidents and executed them with bullets dipped in pigs' blood.† That was how Trump wanted our military to behave, and in his and his supporters' opinion, the last bastion of manhood, the armed forces, had fallen victim to the same "pussification" plaguing American culture.

That line of criticism began in July 2015 when he attacked Arizona senator John McCain, a decorated war hero and POW who was held captive and tortured for more than five years in the Vietnamese prison known as the "Hanoi Hilton." Trump, who enjoyed five deferments from the Vietnam War, referred to McCain in an-

---

* "Donald Trump Wants to Bring in Torture 'Much Stronger Than Waterboarding,'" Canadian Broadcasting Corporation, February 2016, cbc.ca/news/world/donald-trump-torture-waterboarding-1.3452657.

† Tessa Berenson, "The Real Story Behind Donald Trump's Pig's Blood Slander," *Time*, February 24, 2016, time.com/4235405/donald-trump-pig-blood-muslims-story.

swering a question at a leadership summit by saying, "He's not a war hero. He was a war hero because he got captured. I like people who weren't captured."

Many expected this to be the end of Trump's candidacy, myself included, but what we failed to realize then was that Trump had tapped into something visceral and complicated in the country's masculine consciousness. The divide between the idealized military and the actual armed forces—the myth of the Greatest Generation and the opposing reality—has created room for criticism when soldiers and veterans don't live up to the image of invincible and unbeatable warriors. McCain's service and bravery were remarkable, but his courage was in the face of adversity instead of in the aid of victory. His story is unique to the Vietnam War, a conflict whose failure has left succeeding generations feeling emasculated and insecure.

"We don't have victories anymore," Trump told a crowd in Franklin, Tennessee, in October 2015. "We don't win anymore . . . prior to Vietnam, we never lost a war, right? Vietnam was a loss, nothing else you can call it. And then, after that . . . now we don't even think about winning. We lose in Iraq, we lose with ISIS . . ." And when he got to the subject of the generals in charge of the wars we were losing, insinuating our difficulties originated from our military brass's being too "nice," he returned to one of his favorites: "I don't really want a nice general. Bring back Patton. No, seriously."

As we've seen, the division between the Greatest Generation and the Baby Boomers, and how masculinity had changed between those generations, is exemplified by General George Patton. In this version of reality, the one held by Trump and his supporters, the reason why the United States is struggling is because something fundamentally changed in the order of things. "Make America Great Again" translated easily to "return the country to what it once was," and in this case that's a nation where men were men and women and minorities knew their place. "Political correctness" and "progressivism" are simple codes for the means by which white men were being robbed of their rightful power, the rules of society dangerously subverted.

Trump succeeded because he is the personification of white American masculinity. His gruff demeanor, constant threats, boasting about his money and power, his wanton promiscuity, his propensity for blatant cruelty, and his bullying of opponents, which was like something out of a schoolyard socialization, are all traits we've come to associate with men in this country. For lack of a better term, he is the ideal alpha male to anyone with a traditional worldview. He never apologizes, never admits weakness, and is always ready to fight. It's telling, though, that anyone who doesn't buy into the act sees before them a tragically insecure person whose bragging fails to hide his neuroses. For those of us who have been surrounded by men whose arrogance is obviously overcompensation, who talk at length about their money, power, and prowess while exposing their insecurities for the world, you cannot help but see the same in Trump.

The problem is that Trump is himself a reflection of traditional masculine culture. When men steeped in the patriarchy see him, they see themselves. If he's buffoonish—and he most certainly is— then that means that they must also be buffoons. If all of his swaggering egotism is ridiculous, then they must also be ridiculous. If this so-called billionaire who flies in private jets bearing his name, who is married to a model, who lives in a garish tower, isn't the epitome of what men can achieve in America, then what is this system they've all been buying into?

They voted for Trump for the same reason they spend their hard-earned money on massive trucks and jacked-up lawnmowers and Harley Davidsons decked out in expensive chrome. Wearing a Make America Great Again hat means they don't care if they hurt your feelings. Feelings, after all, are for women. They don't care if it offends you. They don't share your worry because worrying is for pussies.

Donald Trump is just another product to supplement their masculinity.

———

It's important, before the consequences of the so-called crisis of masculinity are reviewed, to examine the causes. Besides his most obvious lies, which are all manufactured to save himself from emasculation or legal consequences, Donald Trump's message has resonated with large swathes of the country because there is, at its heart, a kernel of truth. The America he's speaking to, that of my family and others like them, is indeed suffering. When I go home I see a town that's struggling to adapt to changing economic trends. Young people who face a less promising future than their parents have to decide between taking on a massive amount of student debt or risk being left behind. The downtown is shuttered. The school struggles to staff classes. Homeowners are under water and those lucky enough to have jobs are often debilitated by injuries and illnesses they can't afford to treat. Others have fallen victim to prescription drugs designed for addiction. Some turned to heroin, and some have died or become another statistic in a growing number of HIV/AIDS infections that have followed in the epidemic's wake.

As national politicians continue to be bought and sold by billionaire donors and international corporations, the heartland of America gets the raw end of the deal. For generations they've been manipulated by political rhetoric that has consistently deflected blame by telling them that minorities are a threat and have abused the system to their own gain. Turn on Fox News any time of the day and you'll likely find a segment intended for just this purpose. That network and the political party it services have relentlessly hidden their true agenda of increasing the wealth gap and favoring foreign interventionism, both of which harm their voters more than any other group, by pounding away at societal divisions, be they gendered, racial, or xenophobic.

This manipulation has perpetuated an illogical relationship between working- and middle-class Americans and the Republican Party for decades, and that relationship has always been precipitated by a lack of political imagination. Whereas the Republican Party tells its voters there is a limited amount of resources available and appeals to their worst instincts in the division, it could instead be framed that the available resources could be grown if only there were cooperation between the demographics pitted against each other.

What makes this misdirection possible is the battlefield that is mass media. The programs we consume, the advertisements we're fed, the entire mythical life of the United States of America is premised on the falsehood that if anyone else succeeds they're doing so at your expense. When patriarchal men watch television, they've been trained by conservative media to feel attacked. They see one entertainment after another that is constructed with an eye toward diversity and proof that their dominance is threatened. The commercials that air between scenes either promote progressive values or else pepper them with reminders that they must buy the right combination of products or else they're not really men. They can't even turn on an NFL game on Sunday and relax because African American players are taking a knee during the National Anthem and nearly every play is overshadowed by talk of tragic brain injuries. For these men, the click of the remote is all they need to believe they live in a world driven by an Us vs. Them conflict they are losing by the day.

They're justified in feeling that something has changed. The world really is transforming around them, and with those changes their advantages are rapidly evaporating. Industry is giving way to a new economy that favors creativity and communication while rewarding empathy and education, which men are taught to oppose. The future is geared for so-called feminine values, and the education and the democratization of mass culture does mean that minorities who have been held back in the past are now realizing more social and economic potential.

The truth is, the very people who claimed to help men have failed them. Conservatives have won elections by appealing to traditional values and have left working and middle-class men in the lurch by not preparing them for the economic future. The goal was always in cementing the past in the present instead of planning for the future. Republicans lied to men by telling them their factories were coming back. They lied to them by telling them the mines they worked in were going to be reopened. They told them to resist even the most commonsense gun control as their children were murdered in their classrooms. They told them to hate higher learning when all the studies and all the books told the same story: the times were changing and you'd better change with them.

Even more tragically, change has always been in their best interest. The occupations they cling to so desperately—the factory jobs, the mining jobs, the manual labor jobs—were awful in the first place. Men who toil in these careers are underpaid and miserable. They suffer horrific injuries, die prematurely, and are exploited by companies that hardly ever reward their labor or loyalty. But men have long fallen for the great myth of American capitalism.

They strive to make it and when they fail they find solace, no matter how dismal, in their pursuit and their work.

They've been tricked, and to admit now that the lie isn't real, after generations of buying into it and basing their identities on a fraudulent and faulty worldview, would be one of the greatest emasculations ever.

And so they double down nearly every single time.

We've seen this play out in the aftermath of Trump's election. We saw it in Alabama where Republicans stood by Roy Moore as he was accused of statutory rape of underage girls and then when Brett Kavanaugh, Trump's pick to replace Anthony Kennedy on the Supreme Court, was accused of attempted rape and sexual assault by credible victims. In each case, with Moore to an electoral loss and Kavanaugh to his confirmation to the highest court in the land, we watched men attack women as opportunists, as being too unattractive to be violated, as motivated by political and economic ends, because each conflict was another battle in the escalating war in the crisis of masculinity. No ground can be given to the forces of progress here because with each case of men being held accountable for their actions the whole house of cards could come tumbling down. Trump himself seemed to be referencing this when he said of the Kavanaugh controversy, "It's a very scary time for young men in America."* He might have been referring to the possibility of men being falsely accused, which is a statistical rarity, but he might as well have been talking about the anxiety men within the patriarchy are feeling as to the rapid decline of their constructed power system.

It's as if his base of men and their past misdeeds are stand-

---

* Jeremy Diamond, "Trump Says It's 'A Very Scary Time for Young Men in America,'" CNN, October 2, 2018, cnn.com/2018/10/02/politics/trump-scary-time-for-young-men-metoo/index.html.

ing trial with every new instance of public scrutiny and debate. For them, if Kavanaugh, an Ivy League graduate who has enjoyed power and privilege his entire life, can be held responsible for his behavior, then what chance do they have? The Republican Party recognizes this insecurity and has, over time, positioned itself as the lone choice for insecure men who need an ally in the halls of power, even if that means ceding more power to the wealthy in the process.

But again, men have everything to gain by accepting the emerging order. Cooperation between men and women, between the races, between every gender and sexuality, is the only means by which the imbalanced nature of this system can be challenged. But the myth of limited resources and limited results has been damning men to misery and lesser outcomes. It's the lie of no better future, and a play upon their most base insecurities and most terrible instincts, that forces them to cling to their notions of entitlement and the patriarchy that holds them prisoner.

Donald Trump's rise to power was paved with tragic misunderstanding and the resulting anger and frustration. Men refusing to see the patriarchy for what it was and men completely unaware of the patriarchy's existence found a fresh persona and accompanying political movement to reinforce their delusion. Their loyalty to Trump is unending because the fragility of their own masculinity is unending. As long as people like Trump continue to lie and assure them this isn't the case, though, they will never have to face the sobering truth that the problem isn't some external threat, but an internal defect.

The problem isn't immigrants seeking a better life.

The problem isn't minorities fighting for fairness.

The problem isn't women struggling for equal footing.

The problem has always been men trying to hold them down.

14

A few weeks ago one of my relatives stopped by my mom's house to chat for a few minutes and ended up staying for nearly two hours. He's been known to talk someone's ear off, and in the process tell a few stories no one believes. Among the rest of the family, he's actually considered one of the more sensitive guys, someone who can barely contain his emotions and tends to treat people affectionately and kindly. But, in so many ways, this visit was different.

To my mom's disbelief, he talked almost nonstop about mass conspiracies and the decline of the country. The recent spate of school shootings had been hoaxes perpetrated by shadowy individuals trying to take guns away so they could invade America. That conspiracy, he seemed to imply, included efforts to make the next generation of children weak, including sparing them from beatings and denying them discipline, thus ensuring the future would be "a mess." He said his partner didn't want him physically disciplining her kids, but he was more than willing to go to jail if it meant correcting them.

Abruptly he switched topics to rant about the Confederate flag and how it was "history, not hate," that he would wave it if he wanted to, even if it pissed people off. He'd gotten onto the subject of increased sensitivity, "political correctness" he called it, when my mom pointed out that Indiana, where they both live, had actually been a Union state during the Civil War. That led him to the subject of women's "having too many rights" and how they "shouldn't be able to talk up." He said they didn't get discriminated against—any pay gap, if there was one, was because men worked harder and other allegations of harassment were overblown—and my mom, who has been harassed and discriminated against her entire life, said that she loved him, but he didn't know what he was talking about.

My mom called me the next day, completely bewildered. "It was like he was a different person. You wouldn't believe what was coming out of his mouth."

Unfortunately, rants like these are becoming all too commonplace in American discourse. The narrative of the Man Under Attack has spread far and wide throughout the country with severe consequences. Insecure men in every state and every town echo the story my relative told, and though the details are often varied, the implication is universal: sinister forces are conspiring to destroy men and the world they have built.

With my family the roots are found in the Baptist religion we were raised on, a faith that framed our daily lives as continual struggles against the forces of evil. In our family Satan was not just a metaphorical construct but a physical embodiment of malevolent forces who could appear from a cloud of sulfur at any given moment, and his schemes always led toward a final conflict between good and evil in the form of the Battle of Armageddon.

Being raised evangelical, I was taught to look for signs of the apocalypse. On the evening news, every disaster, epidemic, war, or economic downturn was proof that the end times were hastening. Our parents and religious leaders told us that we were more than likely going to see that final battle, and that the leader of the forces of evil, the Antichrist, was probably alive and scheming somewhere in the world at that very second.

I saw a good deal of this rhetoric at play with the rise of the Tea Party, which cast Barack Obama as a tyrant and dictator, which played into the hands of evangelical dread, and soon many were claiming he was the Antichrist. Rumors he had been born in Kenya originated in racist thought, and were perpetuated by Donald Trump himself, but found purchase with evangelicals who suspected he might very well be an evil plant charged with destroying America in aid to Satan.

While it might sound ludicrous, to some evangelicals it's the gospel truth. When Barack Obama proposed his Affordable Care Act (ACA), Republicans' calling it "government takeover" reached an audience ready to believe it was akin to the oft-rumored and feared "Mark of the Beast." Being forced to buy insurance, they reasoned, was tantamount to having 666 tattooed across their foreheads. When they heard rumors that Obama might be spearheading "FEMA internment camps" and "death panels," they heard the message loud and clear: the war they'd been promised was nigh.

The villain of this scenario forms the link between evangelicals and others who hold similar, but secular, anxieties. To the religious and the paranoid, the culprit is the New World Order, an international cabal of affluent and evil individuals who plan to supplant America and conquer the globe for their own benefit. To this end, they have created the United Nations in order to prepare one world government that will overrule sovereign states, have continued to challenge gun rights in order to ensure their coup cannot be defeated, and are waging a constant battle to brainwash their future subjects to be docile and obedient.

For people like my family, this organization has been considered a dire threat for decades. As the story goes, hardly a decision is made in politics or world affairs without the heavy hand of the NWO. The New World Order is a convenient antagonist, and considering the clandestine nature of politics, the idea of a covert clique running the show is a much simpler explanation for why things have changed and why the economy has evolved to the detriment of working-class Americans. You cannot prove they don't exist and if you need to vilify someone or a political ideal, all you have to do is link them to the New World Order and the job is done.

One of the most successful executors of this tactic is Alex Jones. His brand of paranoia has made him millions of dollars as it's entered the mainstream consciousness of the country. No doubt my relative was relaying the type of conspiratorial narrative Jones communicates, and has either listened to Jones or gotten the narrative secondhand from one of his friends or coworkers as his paranoid rantings have infected public discourse. In Jones's daily broadcasts he claims mass shootings are staged events meant to annihilate the Second Amendment, the New World Order is plotting against America, and if they have their way they're going to enslave citizens in a technology-aided dystopia. The forces at work, according to Jones, are "satanists," "pedophiles," and "psychic vampires" aiming to cull the population, indoctrinate children, and turn otherwise strong opponents into "zombies." These plots include furthering the progressive feminist movement, thus destabilizing the culture, and promoting the homosexual lifestyle to reduce procreation and undermine the masculine ideal.

Jones, who enjoys regular communications with Donald Trump,

has a nightmarish vision of America, and his influence has been so great that Hillary Clinton had to denounce him by name in the run-up to the 2016 election. The paranoia he peddles affects national politics, but the show itself is only a vehicle for selling insecurity; his methods are as traditional as what we see on broadcast television. Jones is telling his listeners, the vast majority of them men, that they are in great danger of being emasculated. Evil forces are conspiring to take their homes, their jobs, their guns, and will, if given the chance, rape their wives and children, and the only antidote, in Jones's own words, is the "red-blooded" American male. The appeal works because these are men who already question their masculinity and have a choice to make with their wallets. Their failures are either their own or the result of a massive conspiracy beyond their control.

Control is what Jones sells his listeners. The narrative only highlights the problem; it's his products that alleviate the deficiency. For $350, you can go to Jones's store and buy a ten-pack of "Alpha Power," a supplement designed to increase "physical and mental energy" and boost "sports performance." For the low price of $34.95 (regularly $69.95), you can pick up a bottle of "Super Male Vitality." And, if your insecurity is really getting the best of you, drop $49.95 for "Caveman," a brew of bones and cartilage with a chocolate flavor that'll help return men to their "ancient traditions and practices" where there was "no room for weakness."

Jones and others like him perpetuate a subculture of men who believe the end of the world is imminent, and thus sink their hard-earned money into rations of food and water, disaster bunkers, and the mass stockpiling of weapons, which are necessary, after all, if the man of the house intends on fighting off the shock troops of the New World Order like a new-age Rambo. His show, and so many like it, feature commercials with air raid sirens, staticky radio announcements of martial law, and other effects that signify the coming nationwide emasculation. In this fantasy the world may have turned its collective back on masculine men, but soon we'll all rely on those macho heroes who were right all along to survive and carry out courageous insurgencies against our evil oppressors.

Those conspiracy theories are closely tied to the ones that drive white supremacist organizations, including the KKK, neo-Nazis, and separatist groups. The KKK itself began as a post–Civil War outfit whose aims included protecting white women from so-called "black savages," an extension of white male sexual insecurity. Neo-Nazis employ an amalgam of Adolf Hitler's theories and perverted populism to entice disaffected white men to join their ranks. Separatists include militias who are either preparing for the fall of American society or are actively working to induce it by means of starting race wars or disabling the federal government. All three of these divisions have killed and all three have enjoyed record growth in the last decade, in response to both the election of Barack Obama as the first African American president and the siren call of Donald Trump's politics of anxiety and wrath.

Just as the New World Order business posits that a cabal consisting of women, homosexuals, and minorities is being used to overtake America, these extremist groups hold that machinations by these same groups destabilize white, patriarchal rule. In both cases it's the same hero and the same enemy: proud white men standing up to the barbaric hordes of progressive rogues.

To recruit, these groups primarily radicalize dissatisfied young men online. Dylann Roof was one such convert, and in the months leading up to the massacre in Charleston he spent his time huddled over his computer reading racist websites that convinced him African Americans represented an existential threat. In Roof's own writings he argued that he had to do something, and his attorney based his defense on the method of radicalization, saying, "Every bit of motivation came from things he saw on the Internet. That's it . . . He is simply regurgitating, in whole paragraphs, slogans and facts—bits and pieces of facts that he downloaded from the Internet directly to his brain."*

Ironically, this means of radicalization, as Dr. Neil Johnson, a professor at the University of Miami, has found, works almost exactly as the model the terrorist group ISIS uses to find its members.† In both cases, groups in patriarchal societies are reacting to changing times and societal shifts by lashing out with coordinated violence, the medium of social media interaction enabling individuals to perform "lone wolf" attacks because, as Dr. Richard L. Hasen of the University of California, Irvine School of Law explains, "[it] can both increase intolerance and overcome collective action problems, both allowing for peaceful protest but also supercharging polarization and raising the dangers of violence in the United States."‡

Unfortunately, our news media covers crime in this country with a racist slant that attributes murders committed by white people as individual acts and more often than not fails to put actions into a larger context. Spanning from 2014 to January 2018, the Southern Poverty Law Center attributes forty-three murders and sixty-seven injuries to violence by the so-called alt-right, an umbrella term that

---

* Rebecca Hersher, "What Happened When Dylann Roof Asked Google for Information About Race?" NPR, January 10, 2017, npr.org/sections/thetwo -way/2017/01/10/508363607/what-happened-when-dylann-roof-asked-google -for-information-about-race.

† Natalie Wolchover, "A Physicist Who Models ISIS and the Alt-Right," *Quantum Magazine*, August 23, 2017, quantamagazine.org/a-physicist-who -models-isis-and-the-alt-right-20170823/.

‡ Richard Hasen, "Cheap Speech and What It Has Done (To American Democracy)," *First Amendment Law Review*, April 2018, vol. 16, symposium issue.

now encompasses right-wing extremists in the United States.* Seventeen of those murders took place in 2017 alone. This is an epidemic, but it gets even worse when you include radical actors like Timothy McVeigh, a white supremacist who murdered 168 people in 1995's bombing of the Alfred P. Murrah Federal Building in Oklahoma City, and any number of mass shooters who have slaughtered innocents at their place of work or in schools. Instead, we often dismiss acts like McVeigh's attacks and the shootings as aberrations committed by unwell individuals and consistently miss the correlation to toxic masculinity.

The uniting philosophy in these cases isn't religious, but patriarchal. Just as McVeigh envisioned a federal government emasculating the sovereignty of men, school shooter Dimitrios Pagourtzis saw his advances being rejected by a female classmate as a nullification of his masculine sovereignty, leading him to kill ten in the Friday, May 18, 2018, high school shooting in Santa Fe, Texas. Again, as men are taught that emotions are for women and the only acceptable means of communication is anger, their aggrieved entitlement is routinely finding an outlet in senseless violence.

By putting a kinder and gentler face on these movements, the alt-right has gained power and influence by appealing to recruits who might be tempted to join the KKK or a neo-Nazi outfit by presenting themselves as cleaned-up, intellectual alternatives. Richard Spencer, the man who coined the term in the first place, even founded a D.C.-style think tank called the National Policy Institute and tours the country giving pseudo-academic lectures that seek to rationalize white-centered ethno-states. Online they

---

* Keegan Hankes and Alex Amend, "The Alt-Right Is Killing People," Southern Poverty Law Center, February 5, 2018, splcenter.org/20180205/alt-right -killing-people.

appeal to disaffected young men like the ones who'd been members of the forums I frequented in the late 1990s and early 2000s, men who fashion themselves as somewhat sensitive intellectuals but have been desensitized by years of macho grandstanding, graphic pornography, and digitized peer pressure. The appeal is to assure these men that there is a conspiracy, in this case a politicized alliance, between women, minorities, and "globalists"—a term that has become synonymous with either Jews or members of the New World Order, depending on the situation—to undermine white patriarchal culture, but to do so with an academic slant. Spencer and his fellow leaders present their views in stylized lectures, videos, and memes, and tend to appeal to skewed accounts of culture and history.

In essence, the difference between the new right/alt-right and men who simply support Trumpism because of unconscious needs and insecurities is a question of awareness and ignorance. Those engaged in extremist groups are well versed in the existence of the patriarchal structure and actively seek to reinforce and perpetuate its advantages while other men simply benefit from its privileges despite their obliviousness. In the former, members recognize the fragility of patriarchal rule and are attempting to protect it from social progressivism, while the latter have never considered the artificiality and see all attacks as evil and unnatural.

As Donald Trump rose to national prominence so, too, did the alt-right, and the group became a fixture in political discussions as Trump's own advisor Steve Bannon gave them a platform in both his media company Breitbart and in Trump's campaign. That momentum culminated in 2017 as several factions of alt-right groups, including the KKK and neo-Nazi outfits, converged in Charlottesville, Virginia, to protest the proposed removal of a Robert E. Lee statue. On August 11, they carried torches as they marched through the campus of the University of Virginia and chanted traditional Nazi chants like "blood and soil/blood and soil," before taking to the streets the next day and clashing with counter-protesters in bloody, violent brawls. That day they chanted "you will not replace us," presumably to women and minorities looking to supplant patriarchal white men, before a member of the alt-right plowed his Dodge Charger muscle car into a group of counter-protesters, killing a thirty-two-year-old woman named Heather Heyer and injuring nineteen others.

Though that incident, and increasing public disapproval of the alt-right, hurt their membership, there are still legions of dedicated acolytes, most of them trolls who spend their time on shadowy forums like 4chan and on obscure reddit forums having conversations about murdering liberals, skinning journalists, starting a new Civil War, orchestrating mass genocide, destroying the Constitution and replacing it with a fascist regime, and instituting a new patriarchal order where men are allowed to rape and murder women. It's bewildering to think of how things have changed since the Greatest Generation gave their lives to fight fascism, but fear of the fall of the patriarchy has led to a rise in this ideology.

Members of this disgusting cult often share membership in the "incel" community, where clusters of aggrieved men who are "involuntarily celibate," share this dystopian plan and idolize murderers like Elliot Rodger, and use his picture as avatars and celebrate his birthday and anniversary of his killings while lamenting the state of disproportional power where women can choose not to have sex with them. Between rants about women needing to be murdered or raped, or fantasies of carrying out giant retributive slaughters, these insecure men lament the physical shortcomings they assume precipitate their inability to find love and investigate radical body-morphing processes like "penis stretching, eyebrow botox, wrist enlargement, 'neck training,' nostril shrinking, and 3D printed skull implants."*

Unfortunately, women and society alike pay a terrible price for these insecurities. Recently, an incel named Alek Minassian drove a rental van through the streets of Toronto and intentionally murdered ten people and injured another fourteen, the majority of whom were women.† Before engaging in his attack, Minassian posted to his Facebook wall the following status: "Private (Recruit) Minassian Infantry 00010, wishing to speak to Sgt 4chan please. The Incel Rebellion has already begun! We will overthrow all the Chads and Stacys! All hail the Supreme Gentleman Elliot Rodger!" Minassian has since become a hero among the incel forums, and his name and picture have begun appearing next to Rodger's.

Following that attack *The New York Times* published a controversial column titled "The Redistribution of Sex" by conservative Ross Douthat that began with a startlingly out-of-touch hypothesis: "Sometimes the extremists and radicals and weirdos see the world more clearly than the respectable and moderate and sane."‡ Douthat engaged the threat of incel violence as a market problem wherein the answer might lie in sex robots, sex workers, or, more preferably, by "reviving or adapting older ideas about the virtues of monogamy and chastity and permanence . . ."

Even here, in the case of a man who reacted to fear of emascula-

---

* Jesselyn Cook, "Inside Incels' Looksmaxing Obsession: Penis Stretching, Skull Implants, and Rage," *Huffington Post*, July 24, 2018, huffingtonpost.com /entry/incels-looksmaxing-obsession_us_5b50e56ee4b0de86f48b0a4f.
† "Alek Minassian Toronto Van Attack Suspect Praised 'Incel' Killer," BBC, April 2018, bbc.com/news/world-us-canada-43883052.
‡ Ross Douthat, "The Redistribution of Sex," *New York Times*, May 2018, nytimes .com/2018/05/02/opinion/incels-sex-robots-redistribution.html.

tion by murdering ten people, the onus is on a society "gone rogue." Instead of addressing the aggrieved entitlement of patriarchal men, the solution lies with taming a world wherein women have gained too much independence and autonomy because of advances in freedom and equality. Though Douthat comes short of saying it outright, the article suggests that women have moved past their natural biological and evolutionary role to the detriment of men.

Another voice in this ludicrous conversation is Dr. Jordan Peterson, a Canadian psychologist who toiled in relative obscurity before gaining notoriety in 2016 by opposing transgender nondiscrimination laws. Peterson weighed in on the incel problem in a disastrous profile that also appeared in *The New York Times*, saying the cure for their anger was "enforced monogamy," a turn of phrase that led to outrage among critics who charged that Peterson was supporting an anti-woman dystopia along the lines of Margaret Atwood's *The Handmaid's Tale*.* Peterson defended himself by saying all he had meant was a return to a culture that promoted monogamy as a valued system, but misogynists online agreed the idea sounded pretty good.

Peterson's success—he's become a fixture in sold-out lectures around the world and his books have become bestsellers—is predicated on his theory that the natural order of society has been overturned with disastrous consequences. Again, the villains are feminists and minorities who have weaponized college campuses to undermine the "masculine power of culture," a goal that is antithetical to millennia of tradition and thought. Peterson characterizes these women as "crazy" "harpies" whose more sane sisters need

* Nellie Bowles, "Jordan Peterson, Custodian of the Patriarchy," *New York Times*, May 18, 2018, nytimes.com/2018/05/18/style/jordan-peterson-12-rules-for-life.html.

to step in—because men are not socially allowed to strike women anymore—and stop them before they ruin the world.

A devotee of Carl Jung, Peterson's worldview is grounded in archetypes, or metaphors and stories that have continually reappeared in narratives throughout history. In particular, he focuses on ancient religious texts and maintains that they give us a roadmap of how our society should function. Peterson believes the yin and yang is a symbol for the balance of the world, the white being representative of "order," which he genders as masculine, and the black as "chaos," which he attributes as feminine. In his talks he rants for minutes on end about "the hero," always a male, venturing into the womb of feminine chaos to retrieve knowledge.

Any deviation, he seems to argue, including progressive movements and feminist efforts for equality, are essentially in opposition to the natural order of the world. This gibberish is based on a logical fallacy—Peterson is essentially arguing that the patriarchy should continue to exist because it's existed in the past—but also fails to take into consideration that the texts he cites so often don't just argue for patriarchal rule, they're actually the very texts that established patriarchal rule in the first place.

In much the same way Richard Spencer's propaganda lends pseudo-academic credence to white supremacy, Peterson's work has been adopted by misogynists looking to reinforce patriarchal worldviews with scientific underpinnings and academic rigor. There's a ton of money to be made, for sure, and Peterson has raked in the cash with self-help books that tell men to "take responsibility" and "grow the hell up," a mantra that has been a staple of masculine-focused improvement books for years. Undoubtedly, the same people who shell out thirty bucks for Peterson's *12 Rules for Life: An Antidote to Chaos* also fill their Amazon carts with copies of alt-right figure Mike Cernovich's *Gorilla Mindset*, which instructs them how to "pull" some "hot ass" using confidence and good posture, and Rollo Tomassi's *The Rational Male*, which gives lessons on how to juggle multiple sexual relationships with women like "spinning plates."

Cernovich and Tomassi, and to a similar extent Peterson, have grown in influence and benefited from the growth of a sprawling online community that has come to be known as "The Manosphere." In this misogynistic world, theories like Peterson's academic rationalization of the patriarchy is the norm and nearly every post is dedicated to that pursuit. On one forum, men dissect the "myth of rape culture" and cast doubt on whether women are actually raped as much as research claims. On another forum men discuss how to train females to be their sex slaves via manipulative psychology and emotional abuse. The Red Pill, one of the most popular Manosphere sites located on reddit, functions as an introductory course for men wanting to escape the "lie" of feminist culture and discover for themselves "reality."

In the digital age, the reassurance of fragile masculinity has become big business. Whether it's promoting conspiracy theories that evil forces are just over the horizon or peddling pseudo-science that buttresses the patriarchy, this influx of content and products geared toward insecure men has ballooned as the crisis in masculinity deepens. For the individual, this is all the more reason not to recognize the benefit of casting off the shackles of patriarchy. It means shorter, more miserable lives for men, and for women more rape, more murder, and an environment where men harm them not only because of their aggrieved entitlement but also because of their active denial of that aggrieved entitlement.

And for the rest of the world, it only leads to more generations being hamstrung by an outdated ideology that might have receded if only politicians and charlatans alike hadn't seen a political and financial advantage to selling it to men who should know better.

15

These days I spend a lot of time thinking about generations. Technically, having been born in 1981, I'm considered a millennial, but the difference between my students and me is vast. Sometimes I'll sit in my office, located right off a lounge where the writers hang out, and just listen to their conversations. They're always talking in a strange and unfamiliar way about a combination of real and online life that blends interactions in person and on social media. More often than not their stories focus on internet and phone faux pas that didn't exist when I was younger, whether that means someone didn't like their post on Twitter or hasn't responded to their texts in a timely enough manner.

Our childhoods couldn't be more different. I didn't have the internet until high school and didn't purchase my first cell phone until I was already in college. My first text probably went out in my early twenties. I joined Myspace in graduate school but my page soon became a digital wasteland. Much of my professional life now revolves around social media, but, like all of these other technology-based systems, I've had to study them and learn by trial and error. My students have an instinctual understanding because to them the online world is simply an extension of themselves.

I think that's why this next generation is so different from the ones preceding them. Their lives are split between two separate worlds that feel just as real as the other. Whereas somebody my age looks at the internet or their phones and sees a screen, for millennials the digital space is an existence without boundaries. When they log in they can be whoever they want and project only what they want others to see. Their profiles are meticulously manicured, their feeds maximized for both personal expression and promotion of their own brand, and it's because of this I've always felt that they have an intrinsic grasp of how the new economy works and what it expects. They are their own product—that can be partnered with other products or companies for brief periods of time—but are always in a position for rebranding.

Frankly, that philosophy scares the hell out of me. Having grown up in a factory household where every meal felt like it might be our last, I like having a steady gig and an annual paycheck. When I freelance for publications, the fleetingness of my assignment gives me anxiety. Today I could publish in a large newspaper, tomorrow I could be in the street.

With millennials, so-called job hopping has nearly doubled from previous generations.* Millennials are working for more employers for less time than ever before. In the twelve years I've been teaching, I've noticed a change in how my students talk about their

---

* Guy Berger, "Will This Year's College Grads Job-Hop More Than Previous Grads?" LinkedIn, April 12, 2016, blog.linkedin.com/2016/04/12/will-this -year_s-college-grads-job-hop-more-than-previous-grads.

futures before they ever enter the workplace. They consider jobs as stepping-stones to better opportunities, see every juncture and change as another chance to add to their own skill set and as a means to their ultimate goal, which is almost always more concerned with self-fulfillment than steady employment.

Their careers do not define them, and thus they are less likely to fall for the tried-and-true capitalistic trap. Obviously the market has changed, and with it so have the identities we've always known.

I have a suspicion that much of this comes from the choices that digital worlds offer. I can still remember firing up my first copy of the computer game *The Sims* and struggling to create my initial virtual character. There were a plethora of ways to customize my Sim, so many haircuts, clothing options, jobs, and house decorating schemes to choose from. In the end, however, my Sim more or less resembled myself. Brown hair. Glasses. T-shirt, jeans, and boots.

In those situations I've always felt constrained. The idea of creating an identity that doesn't look like me or live like me is almost impossible. Honestly, it's stressful to even think about a facsimile that isn't more or less the persona I'm currently showing the world. And if that character were to be a different sex? Well, that's a whole other ball game.

Millennials simply don't care. Whenever my students show me their avatars I'm always surprised. Their hair is different. Outfits wildly varied. More often than not they're of a different sex or gender, and in some cases an entirely different species.

This sounds silly, but growing up in a digital playground where nearly anything is possible has given millennials a sense that the analog reality should reflect those possibilities. And in the past, when I watched them experimenting, whether it was how they dressed or carried themselves, there was a part of me that was, quite frankly, a little annoyed.

How dare these people not conform to the standards I'd had to follow.

How dare they find a measure of freedom.

That's the basis of the strife between generations. Already, at thirty-seven, I'm of the age where I can barely stand the popular culture of the day. I've retreated to the music, movies, and television shows of my past and those that harken back to my past experience. But whenever I start getting grouchy about new trends and developments, particularly how earnest and optimistic so much of millennial culture can be, I've learned to take a step back and analyze what irks me, and almost every time it's because that thing represents a conquering of a past frustration or limitation that I'd had to accept. Societal tolerance, in many ways, is based on just that: recognizing that other people can live their lives without subjecting them to the limited truths you've been taught to occupy.

Much of the critique of millennials revolves around accusations of being soft or too emotional, but in truth it's a resentment that we haven't been able to fully explore ourselves without feeling the pressure of society. Because millennials have largely avoided those old pressures, they intuitively understand persona. One morning they can wear sparkling cat ears and the next they might dress up as a lumberjack, and they can be whoever they want or whoever they were born to be without fear of reprisal or rejection. They don't suppress their sexuality or expression of gender like so many of us have in the past.

For myself, and others like me, gender always felt like a fixed lane because as a kid you were bullied and socialized into believing you were subject to the immutable laws of nature. Boys were boys and girls were girls. You liked blue, you roughhoused, you played with trucks, you responded to frustration with anger, and you'd better damn well never cry. Living in a traditionally patriarchal world, that was reality with which there was no arguing. If you deviated it meant there was something fundamentally wrong with you, whether it was a personal defect or, in the case of the evangelical community I grew up in, at the behest of something evil.

Just as Baby Boomers represented a change in the sense of self from the Greatest Generation, millennials have more fully embraced the expression of personal wants and malleability. The duty their parents felt toward society has more or less been replaced by duty to one's own self. They're uncomfortable being labeled, especially with dichotomies like political affiliation or sexuality, because labels represent boundaries that keep them from pursuing their own subjective truth, which flies in the face of societal expectations.

Millennials don't care much for binary anything, and as a result old opinions are quickly falling by the wayside. According to Pew, 51 percent of millennials support gay rights as compared to 37 percent of Generation X and 33 percent of Baby Boomers. Twenty percent of millennials identify as LGBTQ, 63 percent consider themselves allies of the LGBTQ community, and a staggering 12 percent say they are non-cisgender, or do not identify with the corresponding gender of their sex.* In fact, some studies show that as many as half of all millennials consider gender to be on a spectrum.†

To my younger self, the idea of a gender spectrum would've blown my mind. I was taught you had a decision to make, and if you made the wrong one you would receive physical or emotional punishment and risk being ostracized by your loved ones, your peers, and your community. Knowing what I know now, and looking back

---

* "Accelerating Acceptance," GLAAD, 2017, glaad.org/files/aa/2017_GLAAD _Accelerating_Acceptance.pdf.

† "January 2015 Survey of Millennials," Fusion, 2015, fusiondotnet.files .wordpress.com/2015/02/fusion-poll-gender-spectrum.pdf.

over my discomfort as a kid and the hell I went through over the years, I have to believe that had I grown up as a full millennial with an understanding of malleability and that gender spectrum, I might very well be a completely different person.

It's the hardest thing in the world to get over, much like how I still see things at times according to my past religious experience. When I watch the news, much as I did with my family as a kid, a disaster will take place and I'll think, there's a sign of the apocalypse, right there. At a young age the mind is trained how to perceive reality, and even following radical shifts in worldview it's hard to shake, and it breaks my heart to imagine how many people have been forced to live lives wherein they couldn't admit who they were out of fear.

That road is going to be easier for millennials, who live in a society that's actively dismantling the patriarchy. Spurred on by social media, efforts like the #MeToo movement have raised awareness of patriarchal misdeeds and added a new layer of accountability for misogynistic behavior that would've gone unpunished in the past. Economically the gap in workforce participation between men and women is at its lowest since 1948 and a loud and consistent call for equal pay seems to be taking hold.* Women are gaining economic purchase by the day, and men's attitudes are shifting. According to polls of millennials, as many as 88 percent of men say they're fine with a woman making more than them.†

In regard to politically charged gender issues, like the recent

---

* "Women Are Charging Past Men for Jobs in America," *Fortune*, August 16, 2017, fortune.com/2017/08/16/women-employment-work-force-increase/?iid=sr-link1.

† Danielle Paquette, "The Stark Difference Between Millennial Men and Their Dads," *Washington Post*, May 26, 2016, washingtonpost.com/news/wonk/wp/2016/05/26/the-stark-difference-between-millennial-men-and-their-dads/?utm_term=.6e52bc386ad0.

transgender bathroom debate, millennials are of a consensus: according to *USA Today*/Rock the Vote, 62 percent think people should use the facilities for the gender they identify with.* Debates like the bathroom issue are purely of the moment. Past generations raised with more stringent gender identities and societal expectations are struggling to keep up with the time, but as for the future, it's no question. Millennials are overwhelmingly liberal on social issues and thankfully appear to put acceptance, diversity, and multiculturalism at a premium, and they're challenging every old and tired false dichotomy, including sexual identity and gender.

Young men are learning to cast aside traditional masculinity in favor of identities that are healthier for them and society, and it doesn't hurt, obviously, that this change is economically advantageous. With the fall of manufacturing and labor careers, men are learning to appreciate education and the acquisition of "soft skills," as researchers from Pennsylvania State University and Washington State University found in their study "Millennials and Masculinity." These skills were effectively gendered as feminine in the past and include communication and cooperation, but are now necessary for all workers in current and future industries to succeed.

Like Cordelia Fine's *Delusions of Gender* referenced, men are capable of these "soft skills" if they're given a competitive incentive. Now, in an economy that's left behind brute strength and emotional stoicism, they're having to change in order to keep up, and that's going to lead to a brand-new masculinity that will hopefully be better for everyone. Millennials are not as burdened as generations

---

* Susan Page and Fernanda Crescente, "For Millennials, a Consensus on Transgender Bathroom Use," *USA Today*, August 15, 2016, usatoday.com/story /news/politics/onpolitics/2016/08/15/millennials-consensus-transgender -bathroom-use/88751928/.

past, and they're not as terrified by what it means to color outside the rigid lines of tradition.

In the long run, this crisis of masculinity seems like it's going to improve as old expectations are cast off, but what of the rest of us?

Already we've seen how this problem is costing lives and causing hardship, not to mention a political divide that threatens the very existence of our democracy. Those old ways are so hardwired into past generations and the young men currently growing up in patriarchal homes that it seems nearly impossible to counteract. How do they get better?

Or, better put, how do *we* get better?

———

In March I traveled to Austin, Texas, to participate in the 2018 SXSW festival, a scene, I have to admit, I'm simply not cool enough for. After participating in a panel on journalism in the age of the internet, I wandered around the conference. SXSW is a lot, though, and within a half hour I was overwhelmed by the tech displays, impromptu discussions with disruptors and influencers, and generally in need of a bottle of water and a slice of pizza I didn't need to take out a loan to afford.

I was heading out the door when one of the many digital signs displaying the next round of events caught my attention, particularly the title of a talk: "Inspiring Men to Take Charge of Mental Health." It felt like it had the potential to answer one of the glaring questions plaguing us.

How do you get men to change?

The panel was helmed by Joe Conrad, founder and CEO of Cactus, a marketing and communications agency in Denver, and Jarrod Hindman, Deputy Chief of Violence and Injury Protection for the Mental Health Promotion Branch of the Colorado Department of Public Health and Environment. Their discussion centered on their website ManTherapy.com. Hindman explained that in his position he had seen a public health crisis develop in regard to men ages twenty-five to fifty-four accounting for the largest number of suicides in the United States, and the endeavor was undertaken with the hope of destigmatizing mental health and therapy among guys who practiced traditional masculinity.

Their solution was a character named Dr. Rich Mahogany, a Ron Swanson–like alpha male who espoused the benefits of mental health while engaging in masculine activities like fishing, reading manuals for chainsaws, and chowing down on giant sandwiches. The first video of the presentation featured Dr. Mahogany teaching men how to breathe: "Well, your sonuvabitch boss has you working late or you're stuck behind a 105-year-old lady doing seven in the fast lane . . . Breathing exercises are a subtle but manly way to combat stress and anger. Watch as I demonstrate. Close your eyes and take a deep breath through your nose. Feel your breath travel down your gullet and into your belly. Now. Exhale. Fuuuuuuuuuuuuuuuuuuuuuuuuck. Again. Fuuuuuuuuuuuuuuuck."

The crowd expectedly chuckled and Hindman and Conrad explained that their appeal was based in an effort to redefine the paradigm of masculinity to include taking responsibility for one's own mental health. The strategy was to disarm men by first engaging in typical male banter or surrounding their message with masculine symbols—Dr. Mahogany's office is populated with a dartboard, bowling trophies, and a requisite moose head—and then pivot to a rhetorical case for why mental health fits into the rigid masculine structure. As the tagline "Therapy. The Way a Man Would Do It" implies, the argument here isn't to directly challenge the masculine reality in which Man Therapy visitors reside, but to expand it to include healthier behaviors.

ManTherapy.com provides direct information and supplies both the statistics and the site's rhetorical strategy for anyone willing to look, but for men who might be threatened by the prospect of therapy, there are plenty of manly dressings and appeals. As one meme on the site puts it, taking care of your head is no different from keeping your car in good working order. "A man's engine can occasionally overheat," it reads. "Let's pop the hood." On the store page men can buy t-shirts appropriating typically "feminine" de-stressing concepts like aromatherapy with a campfire and meditation through fishing.

In accompanying materials, the crew behind Man Therapy explains this approach by comparing mental illness to a broken leg, thus changing the impression from some abstract thing having to do with feelings to a physical malady men might suffer from working too hard, an appeal that's startlingly easy to understand and recalls, again, the transition of how we came to understand PTSD in veterans. The means of getting this across, whether it's the decorations in Mahogany's office or a reliance on references to bacon and masculine humor, is what they have titled "manspeak," or the means of communication that men engage in that allows them to communicate without fear of emasculation.

I spoke on the phone with Jarrod Hindman about the campaign and its development, which relied on focus groups, conversations with faith leaders, in-depth interviews with suicidal men, proponents of men's health, and a deep examination of mainstream advertising. The site and its accompanying materials have all been created using appeals marketers have used to influence men in the past, but focus on expanding the definition of what a man can be instead of limiting it.

One of the main groups Hindman said he was concerned with are emergency responders who shoulder a large brunt of the suicide epidemic. According to Hindman the resistance among this group, which often holds particularly strong allegiance to masculinity, is very strong and takes time to counteract, but, he suggested, there is more of a chance of progress if the appeal is made using traditionally masculine logic.

In this case, men who are charged with saving and protecting others are given the foolproof argument that if they don't take care of themselves then there's no way they can take care of others. This is exactly what someone is told when they're awaiting takeoff and flight attendants tell them to first secure their oxygen masks before assisting others. You have to take care of yourself so you can help other people. It doesn't hurt, obviously, that this is wired into the masculine ideal of the caretaker. After all, how can you be an effective husband or father if you're not on solid ground yourself?

Hindman touches on this in a particularly illuminating blog post that appeared on the Suicide Prevention Resource Center website in which he argues that appearing vulnerable or asking for help "demands a great deal of strength. It's one of the manliest things we can do." What Hindman is doing here is engaging with the word "strength," one of the most powerfully gendered words in the English language, and actively working to undermine the central contradiction of masculinity—if men are supposed to be strong, then why are they always motivated by fear?

The answer to that contradiction, and perhaps the antidote to toxic, patriarchal masculinity, might very well be one and the same.

———

Following the surprise outcome of the 2016 election, many experts were left wondering just what the hell had happened. Not only had Donald Trump shocked the political establishment, but the results betrayed a growing, existential problem in our society that seemed both incredibly dire and inexplicable. Liberals and conservatives opposed to Trump were left wondering how nearly 63 million Americans had pulled the lever for a man who was, by all conceivable measures, less prepared for the position and woefully unqualified, both ethically and intellectually. There were several reasons for the outcome, including, but not limited to, disastrous campaign decisions, ineffective messaging, backlash toward political insiders, possible foreign interference, and latent racism and misogyny. But one of the main culprits everyone kept coming back to was the construction of ideological echo chambers that isolated people from differing opinions and reinforced their own in the process.

These echo chambers were made possible by technological developments like mass media, the internet, social media, and the prevalence of cell phone culture, all of which allowed individuals to customize a reality tailored to their viewpoint while quarantining themselves from opposing perspectives. This took place on the left as well as the right, and ensured that people were philosophically separated in the lead-up to the election. Though innovation allowed the chambers to be built, the motivation that fueled them was as old as the human mind itself.

Cognitive dissonance is the holding of contradictory thoughts simultaneously, a condition the brain attempts to reconcile as quickly as possible. This is why, when presented with evidence contrary to your own opinion, you'll most often dismiss the new information out of hand. When examining opposing views, a person unconsciously compares the inconsistencies and weighs further action. In some cases the original held belief is so integral to the person's identity that the information is expelled. This is how reports from trusted news sources can be labeled as "fake news" and never given another consideration while poorly written "articles" from less than reputable sources get held up as gospel truth. However, sometimes the new information is so convincing the original belief is either amended to include the information or else discarded completely.

In this case, the latter is much harder to accomplish. The stringent tenets of hegemonic masculinity are so rigid and have been so continually reinforced by society, in the form of both pressure and actual violence, that men have based their entire identities on a false premise, making the breaking of the paradigm quite difficult. For myself, this is in part why I've struggled so much over the years. I was raised to believe this is the only reality and if I ever turned my back on it that meant I had been emasculated, which tended to insulate me from anti-patriarchal messaging. To even begin overcoming my cognitive dissonance, it took years' worth of therapy, study, and introspection, and perhaps the only reason I was able to do that was because I had constant support and was naturally suspicious of the patriarchy in the first place.

When considering men and the problem of toxic masculinity, I tend to see the groups involved as divided into four separate categories. To begin with, there are the men who live in patriarchal environments and are ignorant of the patriarchy. These are individuals who behave in typically performative masculine ways and have never known anything outside of that world. Back home there are plenty of these men and they believe sex and gender are inextricably linked and that men are men and women are women. Among them are the second category: people like my younger self who are immersed in that culture but have a sneaking suspicion there might be something outside of that dichotomy and would be receptive to alternatives. Third are men who are aware of the patriarchy, whether they were raised in non-hegemonic homes or have gained an understanding through education or questioning, and yet still fall under the sway of toxic masculinity due to ingrained mindsets or the allure of societal privilege. And, finally, there are men who recognize the patriarchy and are actively attempting to reinforce it for their own benefit.

Of these men, the final group seems to be the one that is most steeped in its own cognitive dissonance and is perhaps the most unreachable. Members of this subgroup populate the alt-right, join extremist organizations, and live life as fervent misogynists. They are motivated by the power of the patriarchy and many have found there's a ton of money and profit to be made from peddling reassurance to men in doubt. I tend to think these people are wounded, that their participation is more grounded in a weakness that preys on the fear of emasculation, and I've read enough books by and interviews with ex-members of hate groups that I maintain this belief. I don't know exactly how to reach them, but if those ex-members are any indication, the answer is to be kinder to them than they ever are to others.

Christian Picciolini is one of those men, and has come to the forefront lately with his stories of his life as a skinhead youth in Chicago in order to prevent others from following in his path. In a recent conversation Picciolini told me his joining the skinheads was almost completely due to his own insecurities, and once he was in he used the same rhetorical appeal to recruit others. "Every person we recruited was either broken, angry, or disillusioned," he recalled. "It was largely driven by images of Vikings and warriors, all-male-dominated imagery of power and glory." Again, he likened the approach to ISIS, urban gangs, and Boko Haram, cults fueled by patriarchal insecurity and anger.

When asked how to help extremists, Picciolini has encouraged people to show them empathy and love, both of which serve as contradictions to the extremists' belief that they are endangered and live in a world bereft of care.

Similarly, care is what's going to help men escape the cruel prison of patriarchal life regardless of how immersed they are. For people like myself, I've had to come to terms with my own failings in achieving the masculine model and accept that it was unattainable in the first place. It took the support of loved ones' reminding and assuring me that they loved me despite my failings and shortcomings, not to mention calling me on my overcompensation bullshit, and still telling me it was okay if I wasn't invincible, to even stand a chance of escaping the vicious cycle of toxic masculinity. Realizing I could be vulnerable and that my suffering wasn't a sign of weakness, but actually a display of strength, made all the difference in the world. I may not be a perfect messenger in the battle against toxic masculinity, and have certainly had my problems with it in my days and still have to struggle, and still falter, not to fall under its sway. But any insight I can provide is due only to the help and support I received from people who loved me enough to pull me back from the abyss.

If your husband, father, brother, cousin, or friend is one of those people who either inexorably believes in traditional masculinity or struggles with it from time to time, if you feel safe doing so, carefully remind them that it's okay if they aren't always the stoic patriarch. They're going to be terrified of emasculation, as all men raised in that reality are, but if they know other men feel similarly, if they're assured that their spouses, children, friends, and loved ones aren't going to see them as less of a man if they cry or falter or express affection, they might very well improve.

It's always a possibility because patriarchal masculinity is, at its core, a contradictory lie. Men are expected to be protectors, but how can they truly protect what they don't value? Their relationships are stunted by fear of being too vulnerable or emotional, and deep down we understand that. When we fail at work, when we fail at being the masculine ideal, we know that the expectation was unreasonable in the first place. We hurt as much as anyone else; we just work harder to cover it up. And, if the spell is broken, they'll begin to see light at the end of the tunnel. They'll feel better, their relationships will improve, and perhaps that momentum will set them free.

The idea of strength is essential. As Hindman noted, our definition of what strength entails is directly contrary to what the word means in the patriarchal paradigm. Men lash out and are violent because they feel weaker than their circumstances. They die earlier deaths because they're afraid. The denial of these facts, of these deficiencies, is weakness by anyone's definition.

Returning to the subject of veterans of World War II, which cultivated much of our societal ideal of what manhood should look like, the words of President Franklin Delano Roosevelt still ring true: "Courage is not the absence of fear, but rather the assessment that something else is more important than fear." If their bravery and heroism was simply a natural extension of those soldiers as opposed to a conquering of fear, then is that even courage to begin with? In order to be valorous, doesn't a person need to acknowledge their fear and weakness and then fight on in spite of them?

The key to defeating toxic masculinity is in its very definition. If men are invulnerable, then why are we so afraid and so terribly insecure? If men are independent and captains of our own destiny, then how are we subject to so many external forces? Isn't independence about forging your own way, trends and societal pressure be damned? If we're protectors, then why are we hurting those we're supposed to protect? If our masculinity means we're rugged individuals, then why are we all dressing exactly the same, buying exactly the same trucks, engaging in exactly the same behaviors?

By chipping away at the cognitive dissonance that is patriarchal masculinity, men can see for themselves what they've probably always known. This construct is artificial and dangerous. It fits like an ill-tailored shirt and we can see the damage it does and the hurt it inflicts when we look into the eyes of the people we love. The suspicion is there; traditional masculinity is so fragile that it's always on the verge of imploding. This is why the patriarchy is so ever-present and contains so many rules and consequences. Why else do men overcompensate so wildly and so desperately? It's because they're always just moments away from watching the paradigm crumble to pieces.

Much like what happened with my father, men need to feel like they're not alone. The people who care about them, the people who want them to be better, to feel better, to live better, can help them by reaching out and letting them know that their failure to live up to these expectations is not only okay but an absolute certainty. And let's not for a second underplay the importance of men's assuring other men. We have to stop toxic masculinity in its tracks whenever we encounter it. We have to be braver in calling out other men on their locker room talk that perpetuates rape culture and dehumanizes women. We have to call out other men for homophobia and racism. And we have to talk to each other like human beings with feelings so we can know that intimacy and trust are life-giving and essential if we're ever going to improve.

We must recognize the limiting of reality that patriarchal masculinity creates. This world could be different and so much better, we could address the major problems of our time and seek out a better and more functioning democracy and society, if only we could move beyond our antiquated ideas. We could be safer, we could live longer lives, we could be healthier and wealthier. We could transform this country and with it the world.

Once we've exposed patriarchal masculinity as a lie, perhaps we can create a new breed of men. The spectrum of gender affords so many expressions of the self and that freedom can be intoxicating. Men can be whoever they want whenever they want and those new identities are limitless and much healthier. If men still want to express masculine characteristics, that's wonderful, it takes all types, but the toxic aspects, the dangerous aggression, the reliance on anger and violence, the control and the abuse, need to give way to the healthier and more productive traditional traits, those of the provider and the protector, both of which actually lend themselves to communal well-being.

Men need to be reminded that some things are much, much more important than their fear. The happiness and safety of our loved ones. More fulfilling and longer lives. A world in which people are protected and a more humane future is embraced.

If the appeal can use the language and logic of the patriarchy to dismantle the patriarchy itself, if we can take the masculinity so many men are raised with and expand it to include healthier, more socially beneficial behaviors—including acceptance of expression, appreciation of emotion, tolerance for others, and a general understanding that if men are to be seen as leaders and protectors then that means they have to step up and lead and protect others more vulnerable than themselves—and if we can forge ahead and create a new, healthier masculinity, then perhaps we can turn the tide. And finally, thankfully, make men better.

ACKNOWLEDGMENTS

First and foremost, I have so much gratitude for Dan Smetanka, an editor as talented as he is lovely. Dan believed in this book and wouldn't accept anything but my best. Our work has been one of the great privileges of my life.

Thank you to the team at Counterpoint Press. You humble me constantly with your talent and dedication.

Thank you to Clay Risen, my editor at *The New York Times* who took a chance on my first exploration into the permeation of toxic masculinity in American culture and helped me put to words the suspicions I'd been carrying my entire life.

The introspection and chances I took in this book would never have been possible had I not been supported the entire way by friends, loved ones, and colleagues, not to mention the many people who have challenged and inspired me. Thank you to Stacie McDaniel, Laura Agnich, Ted Brimeyer, Melissa Carrion, Lisa Costello, Peter Davis, Bronwen Dickey, Benjamin Drevlow,

Clayton Haldeman, Jarrett Haley, Celeste Headlee, Sean Hill, Bernie Hoseman, Amanda Malone, Jon McKee, Amanda Miska, Eric Nelson, Christina Olson, Jeffrey Pfaller, Chad Posick, Steph Post, Christopher Rhodes, Robert James Russell, Joanna Schreiber, Amanda Schumacher, Marisa Siegel, Josh Sanburn, Adam Schuitema, Kerrie Sendall, Eric Shonkwiler, Johnathan Stark, Laura Valeri, and Christopher Wolford.

JARED YATES SEXTON is the author of *The People Are Going to Rise Like the Waters Upon Your Shore*. His political writing has appeared in *The New York Times*, *The New Republic*, and elsewhere. Sexton is also the author of three collections of fiction and a crime novel, and is an associate professor of creative writing at Georgia Southern University. You can follow him at @JYSexton.